Inspirational Stories of Hope, Love and Encouragement

To Doris:
You are beautiful
Person and truly
a good friend!
Love Ya!
Pam McCray 7/10/12

Pamela McCray

outskirtspress
DENVER, COLORADO

Inspirational Stories of Hope, Love and Encouragement
All Rights Reserved.
Copyright © 2012 Pamela McCray
v3.0

Cover photo by Randy Ledesma (Reflections Photography)

Outskirts Press, Inc.
http://www.outskirtspress.com

ISBN: 978-1-4327-8948-0

Outskirts Press and the "OP" logo are trademarks belonging to Outskirts Press, Inc.

PRINTED IN THE UNITED STATES OF AMERICA

Inspirational Stories

Acknowledgements

To my Father, Horace Ford, who has always encouraged me in my life. He was always there for me. He encouraged me regarding my writings and told me that I could do it. He took the time to read whatever I sent him, and always gave encouraging comments. He was my encourager, and always told me, "You can do it." Thanks, Daddy.

To my mother, Barbara Ford--my mom was my rock and my inspiration. She was a woman of strength. She instilled in me at an early age to always put my "faith, hope and trust in the Lord." From looking at her life, I learned to press on and never settle for less, always striving to do my best. What an example she was! Thanks, Mama.

To my handsome husband, Joseph McCray Sr., I truly thank God for you. You have shown me by example, not to talk about it, but to go after it and do it. You are the love of my life, love you.

To my children, Terrance, Joel Kenneth, and Joseph Marcus McCray, I just love you guys so much. You all have taught me life lessons and because of that you have made me stronger and a better person. Each of you has encouraged me and each of you has always taken the time to listen to me, and you continue to encourage and support me. When I look at each of your lives, and I see what God is doing in each of you I am so impressed with God's handiwork. I am so proud of you Terrance, Ken, and Marcus. I am so blessed to have each of you as my sons. You, my dear sons, are the best and to Christine and Joseph Lawrence, you guys are incredible. You too have made me stronger and a better person. I truly thank you for that. Love, Mama

To my sixteen grandkids; To my grandsons: Almjermyn, Isaiah, Terrance Jr., Terrell, Terreis, Joey, Julius, Jasiah, Devon, Raymond, Anthony, Joseph Marcus Jr. and Elijah, the newest grandson. You guys are awesome. I have learned a lot from each of you and your love just keeps on coming and coming. I love all the hugs and kisses, and "Are you alright, Grandma?" Your love and concern for me is immeasurable, and I cherish your love. Always dream big! Love you guys, Grandma.

To my granddaughters, Joyciana Marie, Jordan, and Kailyn, I waited so long for you all, and who would imagine that in the same year God would bless me with the three of you. What a blessing. The three of you brighten up my world with your smiles, laughter, giggles, and silliness. Keep on laughing and keep on loving. You girls make me want to do better and you inspire me to be a better person. Always do your best and dream your dreams. Love, Grandma

To my sister, Vanessa Marshall, I just love you and I thank God for you. You remind me so much of Mama. You are a strong beautiful woman, and you have accomplished a lot in your life, but don't stop. Our mother taught us many things, and she showed us by example that you can have life and have it all. Pursue your dream. You are a godly woman and a loving sister. Thank you, Nessie. Love, Pam

To my daughters-in-law, LaWanna, Yazzmine, and Olivia; You young ladies have kept me on my toes! I love each one of you for all that you have shown me. You all are so special to me and when the Lord blessed me with you, He blessed me with treasures, because each of you is a treasure to me. Love, Mom

Timika, as far as I'm concerned, you will always be my daughter-in-law. A huge thank you for supporting me and watching my back, you have no idea what that meant to me. You are very special to me and a beautiful young lady. Love, Mom.

Deborah Hector, I just had to mention you. Every time I would share some of my writings with you, you always encouraged me, and continuously would tell me I should write a book. I listened and here it is! You do not know how much you have encouraged me. Thank you, my friend. Love, Pam

Foreword

This is my very first book, and I felt like a woman giving birth. I am so excited! I am so excited that I can barely contain myself; now that's excitement. I have been working on this book for so long, and some of the stories that I have written in this book go back to 1999. I wanted to get this book out; it is about short inspirational stories of hope, love, and encouragement. You may feel as though you do not have hope, you are unlovable, feel helpless, and at times you don't know how to receive love or give love back. This book is meant to encourage you.

Each character in this book is going through something, has been through something, or will eventually go through something. They feel as if there is no hope for them, and they struggle with life, with the choices that they make, and the choices that they made in the past, which had a significant impact on their lives.

At the end of each story, it will leave you feeling as though you do have hope, you are able to love and you are able to encourage others as well as yourself.

You will fall in love with these characters and you will feel what they feel; you will feel their pain and you will feel their joy. You will find yourself cheering and hoping for the best for some of these characters. You just might find yourself in one of these stories.

Each story or poem in this book was guided by the Holy Spirit. He would give me a thought and from that thought, a character, and from there a story. To God be the glory!

Each story lets you know about the love of Jesus and how He loves you, wants the best for you, and how He wants you to accept Him as your Lord and Savior.

Hidden Secrets of the Heart

"**N**ow a certain woman had a flow of blood for twelve years, and had suffered many things from many physicians. She had spent all that she had and was no better, but rather grew worse. She heard about Jesus and she came behind Him in the crowd and "touched His garment." For she said, 'If only I may touch His clothes, I shall be made well'" (Mark 5:25-34, NKJV).

"Immediately the fountain of her blood was dried up, and she felt in her body that she was healed of the affliction. And Jesus, immediately knowing in Himself that power had gone out of Him, turned around in the crowd and said, 'Who touched My clothes?'

"But his disciples said to Him, 'You see the multitude thronging You, and You say,' "Who touched Me?"

"And He looked around to see her who had done this thing. But the woman, fearing and trembling, knowing what had happened to her, came and fell down before Him and told Him the whole truth. And He said to her, 'Daughter your faith had made you well. Go in peace, and be healed of your afflic-tion' (Mark 5: 25-34).

My heart is breaking, and I don't know what to do or what to say. I heard myself call out and say, "Why, why, why, Lord Jesus, why?" I don't know what answer I was expecting, I just knew that I needed an answer. I desperately needed to hear from God. I found myself seeking out my friends for consola-tion, only to find that no one wanted to console me. It seemed as though I was friendless and running on empty. Again, I questioned the Lord and asked why? I was alone, left all alone with feelings of hopelessness and helplessness.

I sat in despair with so many emotions flooding my mind and heart, with tears streaming down my face, feeling dejected, rejected and hopeless. As misery came upon me, I wondered, now what will I do? I felt motherless, fatherless, sisterless and brotherless. No one understood me, no one un-derstood my pain, and no one understood my loneliness or the emptiness within me. Oh, I tried to put on a smile, act cool, and be smooth. Oh, I was able to laugh for a quick moment and act like everything was cool. But at the end of the day, when night came my way, I was alone with no one to phone, feeling all alone, and not wanting to go on.

I then cried out again and said, "Lord Jesus, why?" I've found out there are times we have to be alone, walk alone, and run alone. There are times when our friends cannot console us. I was sick for twelve years, I went from doctor to doctor, and no one had the cure or the answer. This went on for years and years. I spent every penny I had running from doctor to doctor. Finally, I exhausted all of my finances; I had no one to borrow from. I had nothing. Again I was alone. No one cared about me, to tell the truth, and many had forgotten about me. I found myself at wits end. I couldn't take it anymore. I didn't want to go on living. Why, what was the purpose? What did I have to look forward to? What? More pain, more loneliness, emptiness and being by myself.

For the first time I felt like giving up, calling it quits. I was tired, exhausted. Oh, the pain, the emptiness; my bones waxed old with pain. My heart was sorrowful. Oh, the burden that I carried; no one knew and no one cared. I have nothing now, just the pain in my body that I have to live with. No friends, no money and no family.

Just then, as I cried out 'why, why Lord Jesus, why?' At that moment, outside, I heard a lot of commotion, a lot of noise. I looked out my window with a runny nose and a tear-stained face. I quickly moved to the front door to get a good look. As I opened the door, I heard many voices, all in unison. I heard them call out "Jesus, Jesus, Jesus." Oh, they were all calling on the name of Jesus. Jesus was only houses away from me. The people continued to chant Jesus, Jesus. Just then, I don't know what happened, but I found myself on my front porch and walking down my steps and walking toward Jesus. What was I doing? I could get killed just for coming outside of my house. I have to go on, I have to reach Jesus, no matter what happens, I have to reach Jesus. Oh, my feet seem so heavy, my heart is pounding fast, my legs feel so weak, and my palms are sweaty. Oh, I have to continue on--why does it seem as though Jesus is so far away from me; when he is only a few feet away from me?

Oh, Lord I am scared, I am so frightened. Oh, Father, give me strength, Lord, let these cold stone feet of clay become lighter. The people, the people, they are everywhere. They are all around Jesus. Everyone is trying to get to Him; the crowd is pushing in around Him. Oh, I feel that some people are staring at me! I feel as though they know my condition, as if they know my secret. They know what's wrong with me. On no, I can't handle this; Father help me!

I quickly turn my head from the people that are staring at me. I tell myself, I can't focus on them, I must get to Jesus. With every beat of my heart, every breath that I take and every step, I am taking it in the name of Jesus! I've come too far to turn around now. I refuse to be defeated. I am, I will, I shall continue to move on, move forward, to where Jesus is.

What about you? What has pushed you toward Jesus? What has you fearful? What loneliness or pain are you in? What father is trying to help his son? What mother is trying to protect her daughter? Whose heart is broken as you see your kids struggling? What child has the burden to be a mother to his/her siblings? Whose son or daughter is on drugs, in jail, missing, or has run away from home? Whose husband, wife, father, mother, grandmother, son or daughter is facing a critical medical problem? Who has lost their loved ones? What grandparents have to care for their young grandchildren? Who's homeless and jobless? Who has emotional or mental problems? Who is insecure, angry or unforgiving? Who has been from doctor to doctor? Who is separated from his or her spouse and may be going through a divorce? Who is looking for Mr. Right in all the wrong places? Who, who, who is running, who is rejected, who is dejected, friendless, hopeless, or helpless? Who is an alcoholic or drug addict? Who has abandoned their children? Who is in a marriage, and yet all alone? Who, who, who is crying out with a sorrowful heart, bones waxed stiff in pain, feeble knees, and a tear stained face? Who? Oh, my friend don't you stop, don't give up.

You just keep moving forward. Move forward as the woman did who had been sick for twelve years and all alone. Move forward! You see, as the woman got closer to Jesus, she grew bolder. She said within her heart, *No matter what if I can just touch the hem of His garment. Oh, I can't let this crowd stop me. I have to move forward. I can't let fear stop me, I must, I will, I shall touch the hem of His garment.* I tell you, this woman got bolder and bolder; she pressed her way in with the crowd. The closer she got, the more reassured she felt. She put out her arm and she reached, she was close, but not close enough. She reached again. She said within herself, just a few inches more. She put out her arm, stretched out her fingers, and with a made-up mind, she said no more. I've been in too much pain. I can't take it anymore. She reached and she reached. Finally, she touched His garment. She made it! She did it, she moved forward, she reached and she touched His garment.

Suddenly, Jesus stopped; he stopped right in His tracks. He looked around; He asked "Who touched my clothes?" The crowd was silent. Peter, His disciple responded, "What do you mean, who touched you? Master, in this entire crowd any one of these people could have touched you."

Again, Jesus said, "Who touched my clothes?" The woman moved forward, she opened her mouth to speak, she knew what had happened to her. She stood frozen in her tracks. She opened her mouth and spoke aloud in the crowd, where everyone could see and hear her. She spoke and told of all the things that she had been through in the past twelve years. She explained her condition, how she went from doctor to doctor, how she exhausted all of her money. She stated that for twelve years she was alone, she knew what loneliness felt like. But when she was at the lowest point of her life, she had no money, no family, she had no one. She couldn't take it anymore. That's when she heard her neighbors calling on the name of Jesus.

You see, with everything you've been through, the lonely nights, lonely days, feeling all alone with your innermost pains. I'm talking about the heartaches--you know the ones you carry around with you day in and day out. The pain that has you dejected, the pain that has you frown when you want to smile. The pain about which you want to tell someone but, instead, you carry the pain alone. The pain about which you feel no one understands. The pains that cause you to feel everyone is judging you, the pain that makes you believe you are a failure. Oh, my sisters and brothers. It's time to be like the woman and say, "No more. I can't take it anymore. I too must seek Jesus."

Give your concerns, problems, and burdens to Jesus. The woman spoke and answered Jesus and said, "I did. I touched you." You see, Jesus knew exactly who had touched Him. But at times we have to confess with our mouths and move forward in faith, believing that God is able to take care of whatever is bothering us. After the woman touched Jesus, she knew immediately that she was healed. She then sought to disappear into the crowd. Jesus immediately asked, "Who touched my clothes." You see, as the woman said, "I did," she was openly saying in front of the crowd, *I believe that If I just touched Jesus garment I would be healed. I had faith that Jesus would heal me.* As she publicly spoke, Jesus publicly and openly blessed her.

Jesus said, "Daughter, your faith has made you well, go in peace and be healed of your affliction.

When we move forward in faith, believing within our hearts, we then openly speak. It is at this point that Jesus openly blesses us. He wanted the crowd to know when we seek Him, we will find Him. Jesus will bless us, for all to see the goodness of the Lord.

You may have pain. Only you know of that pain that is tormenting you. I lovingly say to you, "You are not alone." Oh, you may feel alone, but Jesus already knows of your secret pain. Be like the woman and seek Jesus, move forward in faith, believing in your heart that Jesus can heal your pain. We all go through things and don't want others to know how we really feel. We've all had sleepless nights and lonely days. We've all shed some tears. I believe at one time or another we all have had "secret pain." The pain where we could not let others in; we had to deal with it alone. Don't try to carry your secret pain alone. Maybe some of you reading this may not have had a "secret pain." Others reading this may have had or now have a secret pain. Whatever your situation may be, no matter how difficult you believe it is, let me say that nothing is too hard for God. This book may not be for everyone but it is for someone!

My prayer for you is to be free--free from what you are holding on to. Give your secret pain over to the Lord. Is it easy? Yes and no. You have to be willing to give it over to the Lord and you have to confess to the Lord your secret pain and move forward in faith, believing that God can and will change your situation. Only you know what your secret pain is.

Prayer: Lord, Jesus, I give my "secret pain" to You. The

pain that breaks my heart and overwhelms me with sorrow. The "secret pain" where I can do nothing but watch. Father, I give my "secret pain" to you with each tear that has fallen from my eyes, concerning my "secret pain." I freely give it to you.

If you don't know Jesus, but would like to accept Jesus as your Lord and Savior say: Father, I confess my sins to you. I ask that you forgive me of my sins, and I ask that you come into my heart and live. Amen!

Encouragement: Always remember that Jesus loves you. He cares about everything that bothers you. He wants you to give your "secret pain" to Him.

Journey on a Straight Path

"Now the Lord said to Samuel, 'How long will you mourn for Saul, seeing I have rejected him from reigning over Israel? Fill your horn with oil, and go. I am sending you to Jesse the Bethlehemite. For I have provided Myself a king among his sons'" (1st Samuel 16:1, NKJV).

As I prepare for my journey, a journey on this path that is set before me, I must have all the necessary equipment for my journey. You see, I don't know how long I will be on this path, or where this path will lead me. I don't know who I will encounter on this path. What I do know is that I am a servant, a servant of the Almighty God. I have given my life to my Lord and Savior, and only He knows what's on the path that is set before me. But as I prepare to travel on this path, I won't be alone; I will have companionship every step of the way. So do I worry or fear? No, because my companion is Mighty and Strong. My companion can warn me of the dangers that are before me. He can warn of the attacks that are being formed against me. Where I cannot see, my companion sees around me. As I travel this path, I know that I have an enemy who will try to kill, steal, and destroy me. My companion has given me specific instruction for the clothing that I am to wear on this journey. First, I must dress in the Helmet of Salvation. Next, the Breastplate of Righteousness, the Belt of Truth, Gospel of Peace, Shield of Faith, and Sword of the Spirit. Now I am dressed from my head to my toes in armor that my companion has instructed me to wear.

On the first day of my journey, we have not traveled far at all. We ran into an enemy, an enemy called "Doubt." Doubt stopped us on the path and he questioned me about my past. Doubt asked me, did I believe I was born again? Doubt said, you say all the right words, and pray the right prayer, but how do you feel? Do you feel a difference, do you see a change? As I was about to answer doubt in my own strength, my companion spoke for me and He said "If thou confess with thy mouth the Lord Jesus and believe in your heart that God has raised Him from the dead, you will be saved, not might, but shall be saved" (Romans 10:9). As soon as my companion spoke those words doubt was nowhere to be found. As my companion and I continued on our journey, I said to my companion, "Thank you for the gift of salvation, thank you for saving me." Still traveling and feeling self-assured, we walked down this Christian path on this Christian journey.

My companion and I continued to travel down the path; we could see ahead of us, there was a lot of commotion. Soldiers, soldiers, soldiers everywhere, there was yelling, screaming, and taunting. We started to run on the path to get to where the commotion was. My companion was in a hurry. He said He needed to help out his friend. I asked him, what friend? He replied, "Don't worry, you will meet him." As we reached the crowd, soldiers were everywhere. I was able to push my way through to the front of the crowd, I was able to see, and to my surprise, on this journey, on this path, the person who I was about to meet, he was going to show me, that in the midst of your storm, you could have "godly character." Who is this friend?

Let me introduce you to my friend. DAVID: Anointed to be King.

His name means *well beloved*. David was God's chosen one; David was anointed to be King. David had purpose in his life, and a destiny to fulfill. David was given a glimpse of his future. David would be king. But there are some lessons that David had to learn. As for you and I, there are lessons that we have to learn on this journey on a straight path.

Now the Lord said to Samuel "How long will you grieve over Saul, since I have rejected him from being king over Israel? Fill your horn with oil and go, I will send you to Jesse the Bethlehemite, for I have selected a king for myself among his sons" (1st Samuel 16:1). When they entered, he looked at Eliab and thought, "Surely the Lord's anointed is before Him, but the Lord said to Samuel, "Do not look at his appearance or at the height or his stature because I have rejected him; for God sees not as man sees, for man looks at the outward appearance, but the Lord looks at the heart." Then Jesse called Abinadab and made him pass before Samuel. But Samuel said to Jesse, "The Lord has not chosen this one either." Next Jesse made Shammath pass by, and he said, "The Lord has not chosen this one either." Thus Jesse made seven of his sons pass before Samuel. But Samuel said to Jesse, "The Lord has not chosen these." And Samuel said to Jesse, "Are these all the children?" And he said "There remains yet the youngest, and behold, he is tending the sheep." Then Samuel said to Jesse, "Send and bring him; for we will not sit down until he comes here." So he sent and brought him in. Now he was ruddy, with beautiful eyes and a handsome appearance, and the Lord said, "Arise, anoint him for this is he." Then Samuel took the horn of oil and anointed him in the midst of his brothers; and the Spirit of the Lord came mightily upon David from that day forward (1st Samuel 16:6-13).

Can you hang out with David and me for a while on this journey on a straight path, or is the path too straight for you?

My companion and I arrived just in time, not too early and not too late but right on time. As my companion and I stood in front of the crowd, we glimpsed David trying on Saul's armor. David was about to enter into a fight, one-on-one; he was about to fight Goliath. (Goliath's name means "exile," he was a giant of Gath, and he stood nine feet, nine inches tall. He wore a bronze helmet and his bronze armor weighted about 125 pounds, his spear was designed for hand-to-hand combat, like a long sword, the head of this spear weighed about 17 pounds.)

We see David trying on Saul's armor (1st Samuel 17:38-40). So Saul clothed David with his armor, and he put a bronze helmet on his head; he also clothed him with a coat of mail. David fastened his sword to his armor and tried to walk, for he had not tested them. And David said to Saul, "I cannot walk with these, for I have not tested them." (Test means to examine, try or prove). So David took them off. Then he took his staff in his hand, and he chose for himself five smooth stones from the brook and put them in a shepherd's bag, in a pouch which he had, and his sling was in his hand.

I looked at David, and I looked at his enemy. In my heart I knew this handsome young man was not going to make it. I looked at my companion with fear in my eyes; he looked at me and just smiled. I looked at the soldiers all standing around. I heard their whispers, "He's not going to make it, poor guy." Fear gripped me as never before, I looked again at David. What is he doing? What is he saying? What does he mean I have not tested them? Why is he being so particular now at this appointed time? Who is he trying to impress, does he not know I am to go on a journey with him. Does he not know I am to learn from him? The crowd was in an uproar, there was yelling and screaming--the enemy taunting and yelling, I look around again, I see Goliath and his soldiers on one side of the mountain. I see Israel on the other side of the mountain. The yelling and screaming, the noise, it's all so loud. I see fear in the men's faces, they are so afraid. I hear Goliath in a deep thunderous voice saying, "I defy the armies of Israel this day; give me a man, that we may fight together. Oh, I hear the boldness in Goliath's voice. I hear his laughing. He thinks he is invincible. I see no fear in this nine foot, nine inch giant.

Oh, somebody do something. Don't let David go and fight this giant, he can't handle himself. He never fought in a war before. He's going to get hurt. This fight, this giant is too much for David. Look at the soldiers all dressed in their armor, all the war chariots on both sides of the mountains, with the valley between them. Oh, David, what are you doing? Wait, what's that I see? What is that look on his face? What is he thinking? Yes, yes he looks like he's self-assured, but why?

What, what did I hear him say? Did he say, yes, he's repeating himself, he's saying, "Your servant used to keep his father's sheep, and when a lion or a bear came and took a lamb out of the flock, I went out after it and struck it, and delivered the lamb from its mouth; and when it rose against me, I caught it by its beard, and struck and killed it. Your servant has killed both lion and bear; and this uncircumcised Philistine will be like one of them, seeing he has defied the armies of the living God." David further said, "The LORD who delivered me from the paw of the lion and from the paw of the bear, He will deliver me from the hand of this Philistine (1st Samuel 17:34-37).

There strode David, with his five smooth stones, putting his stones in his shepherd's bag and carrying his sling. Yes, I saw David was self-assured--each step was a step being taken by a person who's been with the Lord. His steps were powerful steps, each step toward that Philistine giant were victory steps. What Goliath did not know was that he'd made David so angry by defying the armies of the living God. David's steps were righteous steps; his steps were ordered by the Lord. David said to Goliath, in a voice that was powerful, unshakable, "You come to me with a sword, with a spear, and with a javelin. But I come to you in the name of the Lord of Hosts, the God of the armies of Israel, whom you have defied. This day the LORD will deliver you into my hand, and I will strike you and take your head from you" (1st Samuel 17:45-46). The fight was on, and it intensified. The soldiers were yelling, screaming, and the noise was so loud that even the horses were bucking. I heard Israel's soldiers saying, "Go David, go David, go David, go..." I saw David, he was in the valley drawing near to Goliath, and Goliath was drawing near to him. I could hear David's voice over the crowd saying, "Then all this assembly shall know that the LORD does not save with sword and spear; for the battle is the LORD's and He will give you into our hands" (1st Samuel 17:47, NKJV).

David was taking off-- running, running toward the army to meet this Goliath. Oh, I glimpsed him putting his hand into his bag, he was taking out a stone, then he slung the stone. What, oh my, the stone struck Goliath in his forehead; the stone sank into his forehead; Oh that giant fell on his face to the earth. One stone and a sling--that's what David used. David won the fight. That giant, big as he was, didn't have a chance. David won his battle, but not in his strength. David won the battle depending on God. David's words "the battle is the LORD's" put this contest into proper perspective. David knew his steps were guided by the Lord. David knew that God would deliver his own against overwhelming odds. On this journey on a straight path, my first lesson from David: no matter how big the giant may be or how thunderous his voice may sound, the battle is not mine, it's the Lord's. To put your faith and trust in the Lord, depend on God as your defender. No matter what the odds may look like, you must be confident that God can deliver his own against overwhelming odds. To God be the Glory!

There may be a Goliath in your life, are you willing to let God fight your battle for you? Will you run toward your Goliath or run from your Goliath? Learn from David and know your Goliath can be defeated. Trust God with your Goliath.

Are you still with me on this journey on a straight path

or have you fallen by the wayside? I must warn you now; you may want to stop reading now. As David and I continue to travel on this journey on a straight path, we will encounter traps, ambushes, and decoys that the enemy has set for us.

ARE YOU READY?

David was anointed King, even before he fought Goliath. But when the Lord gives you a glimpse of your future, gives you a vision, calls you by your name and shows you your destiny, do you think for one moment that you are going to walk straight into your destiny? You see, on this journey on a straight path, you will encounter many things; you will go through a process before you reach your destiny.

Come, follow David and me and see what lessons we will learn along the way along this journey on this path. As we traveled down this path, I looked for my companion. I thought I lost him in all of the confusion, but he was right here in the midst of David and me. David started to tell me how he used to play an instrument for King Saul, and how his music would soothe the King. He also told me how King Saul set him over the men of war, and gave him his daughter to marry. David was leading the men in war and enjoying his time at home with his wife.

David went on to say that one day something unusual happened. He said, "When he and King Saul were returning from war, that the women had come out of all of the cities of Israel, singing and dancing to meet King Saul with tambourines, with joy and with musical instruments, so the women sang as they danced. David stopped what he was saying, he looked at me with amazement in his eyes, and he continued. The women sang, "Saul has slain his thousands, and David his ten thousands." I stopped in my tracks, my mouth wide open, eyes bugged and I said, "No, no they didn't, they didn't sing that, did they?" David continued, "Yes, and after that King Saul became jealous of me, and wanted to kill me."

That's when he had to run away from King Saul. I could hear anguish in his voice. I felt so bad for him. He was so happy and now he was running for his life. He had to leave, David continued, he had to leave his wife, his parents, his friends, not to mention all the luxuries he had come to enjoy. He said, "I've never seen a person so full of hatred. How could love turn so fast into hatred? I've never felt such resentment, anger, bitterness and jealousy from one person. The king had so much bitterness and resentment that I had to run for my life, I had to run to this cave, this cave called "Adullam." Oh, how my heart goes out to David, as he continued to speak, I saw his eyes filled with tears. I saw that this new friend of mine, David, was a compassionate young man. As David entered the Cave of Adullam (1st Samuel 22:1-2), he entered into this cave a broken man, a rejected man, a man who was feeling worthless, a man who felt he was being persecuted, and a dejected man. As I continued to watch him, I saw he was lonely, and had low self-esteem. He'd been lied to, mistreated, talked about and deceived. You see, on this journey on a straight path, David had come face to face with the enemy, who was trying to kill him, destroy, him, steal from him and yes, even hinder him from what he was called to do. David stared at me, and he began to speak very softly. "Pam, while you're on this journey on a straight path, you, too, will find that along the way you will meet people-- people like King Saul and they will resent you, envy you, and reject you. You will have people who will have bitterness against you and be angry at you. Pam, yes, you will meet people who even have hatred for you. You will be lied to, mistreated, talked about and despised while on your journey."

I looked at David with fear in my eyes; my heart was pounding harder and harder. I felt the beads of sweat fall from my forehead. I wanted to speak; I wanted to ask David, why, why, why would I encounter all of this? I moved my lips, but the words, the words oh, oh, God, the words wouldn't come out of my mouth. My throat, it was so dry, so dry. I felt the tears--tears streaming down my cheeks. I looked at David again, yes, yes, now I hear myself. I hear myself saying the words, "Why, why, why, will I encounter all of this? David, answer me, answer me, answer me, David. Why, why? I'm a Christian just trying to do the right thing on this journey on a straight path."

David looked at me and said very firmly, "Pam, you too have an enemy who's trying to kill, steal, destroy you, and even hinder you on the journey on a straight path." David stopped speaking; he glanced at the entrance of the cave. Apparently David's father's house and his brothers heard what happened to David, and they went down to the cave with David. Everyone was in distress. Whoever was in debt and discontented, gathered to him. So he became their Captain, leader over all of them and there were about 400 men with him. What David did next astonished me. He called all of the men together; he began to speak boldly and said, "I know all of you men are not here to support me, but the reason you are all here is because you are discontented with King Saul's rule, and you are debtors, oppressed and troubled. So, you heard what happened to me, and said to yourselves, 'I'll go with David.' Well, that's fine. I don't have a problem with that, but I must warn you, if you stay with me on this journey on a straight path you will encounter some things. You see, when I was a young man, the Lord gave me a glimpse of my future, and I have a destination that I must get to. I don't know how long I will be in this cave of Adullam. But I know I have a purpose. Nothing is going to stop me from fulfilling what God has called me to do. There are some lessons I have to learn along the way. You see, I felt rejection, bitterness, envy and jealousy. I came face to face with hatred. I know firsthand what it feels like to be lied on and mistreated. I must continue to warn you, if you stay on this journey with me, all of us will encounter mistreatment; we will feel the bitterness, jealousy, anger, and hatred from our enemies. We will experience the loneliness." The men looked at one another, and then one man came forth and said, "David, we know you are to be the next king, and you know what type of men we are. But yet, you stand there and warn us of the danger and traps that are before us. David, we know you are a man of compassion, and a godly man. We will go and be with you. You are our leader. Whatever process you have to go through, we will go through with you." David said, "Men, there will be some hard times ahead of us." All the men looked at David and each man, one by one, gave his yes!

David was overcome, and he began to pray, "I waited patiently for the Lord, and he inclined to me, and heard my cry. He also brought me up and out of a horrible pit, out of the miry clay, and set my feet upon a rock, And established my steps. He has put a new song in my mouth, Praise to our God, many will see it and will trust in the Lord (Psalm 40:1-3, NKJV).

I stood there in amazement; what I had just witnessed was unbelievable. These men were willing to follow David, even in his time of distress and time of trouble. What David began to do was teach his men; David poured himself into his men. David came to love his men and his men loved him. While in the cave, David was still running for his life, but he was learning while he was in the cave. David learned how to overcome rejection, hatred, envy, strife, jealousy, low self-esteem, resentment, deception, and deceit.

On this journey on a straight path, David knew he had a destiny and a destination. David knew that while he was in the "Cave of Adullam" that God was preparing him. David knew he was being tested and he had to learn what God wanted him to learn. He knew he would still encounter rejection, loneliness, and jealousy. But David had to learn as a leader how to deal with rejection, anger, bitterness--how to deal with these things in wisdom.

You see, God was doing a great work in David. God was showing David that as a leader you have to learn people and their ways. You have to know who you can and cannot trust. David learned this lesson well, and became the next King.

David looked at me, and said, "Pam, I came into this cave, the Cave of Adullam, depressed, rejected, with self-pity, lonely, feelings of worthlessness, being resented, lied about, mistreated, talked about, envied, and persecuted. I came in a broken man. But it's time for me to leave this cave, and it's time for us to separate our ways."

"Oh, David I cried, I came on this journey on a straight path to learn from you. I saw the way you came into the cave. I saw the way you turned to God in the cave. I've learned so much from you and your ways. I see you emerging out of this cave as a strong leader, a man full of compassion, a godly man, vibrant, self-assured, and undefeated--a man with a vision, and a man with purpose in life. David was being prepared for destiny while in the cave. Yes, it's time; time for us to depart our ways, there's so much more that I have to learn on this journey on a straight path. But as I leave, I leave with peace and wisdom. Thank you, David." With tears in my eyes, I looked at my companion who was with us all the while. He whispered to me so softly and sweetly, and He said, "I'm here, right here with you, as He pointed to my heart, He said, "I will never leave you nor forsake you." (Hebrews 13:5).

To God be the Glory!

If you are in your "Cave of Adullam," God is building character in you. If you've been lied to, talked about, mistreated, stepped on, thrown aside, forgotten, misused, wronged, abused, slandered, envied, or rejected, I say rejoice. Why? Because you are God's chosen one, His anointed one. He called you by your name, he lifted you up, and He kept you His secret until the appointed time. The things you went through were to strengthen you, to make you stronger, for you to endure, to stand, to be fit for the master's use. If you have a destination, a place to be at an appointed time, start learning your lessons now.

You have to learn through your pains, your tears, and your heartaches. You have to learn to conquer fear, loneliness, deceit, and doubt. You have to learn to see God anew, afresh. You, yes you, God's anointed one. You have a purpose, you have a destiny, and you must reach your destination at the appointed time. Even if you have to crawl on the path that God has set before you, you have to learn to take it baby steps at a time. You have to learn how to walk the path God has set before you. Then you have to learn how to run the race God has set before you.

As Paul stated, "I reach for the prize, forgetting those things that are behind me and running the race set before me (Philippians 3:13-14). You see, you must forgive the ones that talked about you, lied about you, mistreated you, abused you, hated you, and the ones that are jealous of you. The ones that didn't care for you and whose hearts were hardened toward you. These things are behind you.

Keep your eyes on the prize; you must be able to forgive. The choice is yours, you can be set free, and it's up to you. Go to God and release that person or persons to the Lord. Choose to forgive that person. You must move forward. Don't let the enemy hinder you. Pray for those who have mistreated you, release that person to God.

Do not take the winding road; choose to stay on this journey on a straight path, live victoriously, forgetting those things that are behind you, reaching for the prize. You have a purpose. You have a destiny. You must reach your destination at the appointed time. Learn from David. May God bless you on this "Journey on a Straight Path."

The Power of Love

There was a groom, and he was to be married to his beautiful bride, but before they took their wedding vows, the groom had to confess something to his bride.

"You know how much I love you and want you to be my wife, but before we take our vows, I want to tell you something." He began by telling her how much he loved her. As he looked into her big brown eyes, the words began to flow, "For you to fully understand what I am about to say, let me take you to another time, to where it all began.

"When I was a young boy, growing up in my father's and mother's house, living with my two brothers and my two older sisters, we had responsibilities, we had chores we had to do around the house. For our schooling we had study time in the evenings; and on weekends, my brothers and I had to tend to the yard, cutting the grass and the hedges, and edging the yard. We also had to do our neighbor's yard. On Sunday, we went to church as a family, came home and had dinner.

"I began to get tired of this routine; it began to be a drag.

Across the street from me lived a boy four to five years older than I, and his name was Jack. He looked like he had it going on. I began to watch him, and as I watched him, I could see his lifestyle was different from mine. He could come and go as he pleased. He didn't have to work the way I did. He did whatever he wanted to do.

One day Jack approached me; it was on a Saturday afternoon and I was working in the yard. Jack looked at me and said, "Man, I see you watching me all the time. Why do you watch me like that?"

I replied, "Jack, I see you all the time, you come and go as you please. I don't ever see you do any yard work. I see your dad cutting the grass."

Jack responded, "Yeah, I don't have time for all that. My pops, he does all that stuff. Hey, but since you've been watching me, you want to hang out with me and my partners? Hey, you can become one of us."

"Well, I don't know. I have a lot of responsibilities here at home."

Jack shouted out, "Well, stop watching me all the time. See, me and my boys we got it going on. We all hang together; we don't answer to no one. But you ain't ready to be a part of us. See you later man."

I hollered after Jack, "Hey, Jack, wait! What do I have to do to become a part of you guys?" Jack shouted back, "First, you have to prove to us that you got what it takes to become one of us. Tell you what; meet us tonight at eight o'clock at the youth club, hey, if your daddy lets you out." (Ha, ha).

"I'll be there at eight tonight, I'll be there." For the rest of the day I was excited, I was about to belong. Oh, I was going to be there at 8:00 and no one was going to stop me. I didn't know what I was going to tell my dad. I only knew I was going to meet Jack and the rest of the guys that night. Well, 7:30 came, then 7:45. My dad was not home yet, so I asked my mom, "Could I go to the youth center to shoot some hoops?" she said yes. Mom told me what time to be home.

Before I left the house my mother called me, "Junior, are you ok? You seemed to be restless all day; is everything alright with you?"

"Yeah Mom, I'm fine, nothing going on with me."

"Okay, she replied, "but if you want to talk, you know I'm here for you."

"Yeah Mom, I know, but, like I said, everything is fine." I left, saying to myself, *She must know something.* I made it to the youth center; Jack and the guys were there. Jack began, "Hey, Lil dude (that's what Jack called me), I didn't think your daddy was going to let you out." They all began to laugh. "Well, I'm here now, so what's up?"

Jack introduced me to the gang. I'd seen these dudes hanging out on the streets and ditching school.

One of the guys stepped out and said, "If you want to become one of us, you going to have to prove yourself. Do you think you can prove yourself?"

I yelled out in my toughest voice, "Prove myself, prove myself how? Man, what are you talking about?"

What came out of his mouth frightened me. I was full of fear, but I couldn't let them know I was scared. I wanted to become one of them.

He said, "You see the ten of us here tonight? Well, what we do is take you to a secluded area, and rush you."

"Rush me, what does that mean?"

Someone said "Lil dude, you sound like you're scared. Look at you, you are scared."

I yelled back, "Man, I ain't scared; just tell me, what does it mean?"

Jack started, "Like my man here said, we take you to a secluded area, and we all beat you, jump on you, whip the stuffing's out of you, to see how much you can take and if you can take it. Are you game? Can you hang, Lil dude?"

In my mind, I was saying, *I don't know what I've gotten myself into, but how do I get out of this or can I?* Just then my lips moved, and I heard myself say, "Well, I am here now; let's get it on, I'm ready." Well, you can imagine the rest, we all went to a secluded area, the initiation began. When it was all over with, that night I was one of the gang. I had made it, I was in, I was one of them and I belonged.

At home, things began to go downhill, I began to stay out late; my grades went down, I became so rebellious. One day, my two brothers cornered me. They began, "Word out on the streets that you're in a gang; you went through with the initiation and everything."

I looked at my two brothers, I pushed out my chest, and I said in my toughest and roughest voice, "Yeah, I'm in with the fellas; what's it to you?"

My two brothers said, "We are going to show you."

I was ready for them, if I was able to hang out with ten guys, who were these two? I yelled out, "Well, what you gonna do?"

I was stunned at what they did; tears came rushing and streaming down my face. In all my toughness and my hardness, I was crying like a baby. My two brothers only hugged me and said, "Junior, we love you, we don't want to see you get hurt." They began to talk, not at me, but to me. In my brothers I've seen a brother's love. I listened to what they had to say, and I respected them for being honest with me, but in the hardness of my heart, I didn't get out of the gang. In fact, things got worse.

At home, there was tension in the house. My father came home from work one evening and he called for me. "Junior!"

I came down the stairs, my father looked at me, and said, "I hear that you are in a gang, you're out there in the streets acting wild. Sit down, Junior. Out there in the streets is only trouble. In the streets you can get hurt. Junior, you don't know that out there in the streets, in the blackness of the night that everyone out there is looking for something. In their own way they are trying to cover their own hurts and pain. They are all out there looking for something, mostly, looking for love and to fit in. But, Junior, you have me and your mother that love you and want the best for you. Your brothers and sisters love you, Junior, and want the best for you. I love you Junior, and I am here for you. I've always been here for you. You have to follow our rules and get out of that gang."

"But pops, I can't just get out like that, I can't walk away from them, do you know what will happen?"

"Junior, you can get out, there's no such thing as can't."

I looked at my dad for a moment, and said "No, Dad, I won't get out, I won't."

"Well, Junior you leave me no choice; you cannot stay in my house, disrespect your mother and me, disrespect your brothers and sisters, let your grades go down, come in whenever you want. It stops, and it stops now. Junior, I love you, son, but I cannot allow you to bring destruction to our home. I cannot idly sit by and watch you turn into something--something that is not you. I've raised you the best way I've known. I've worked to put a roof over this family's head, provided for your needs. Junior, I've done the best that I could. No, I'm not perfect, but I was a loving and supportive father. I did my best."

Junior interrupted his father by saying, "Yeah, Dad it's time for me to leave, to learn some things on my own. Just remember, you're the one that's putting me out. No, Dad, don't answer that, because I am gone, you don't have to worry about me, I am seventeen years old, and I am a man, yeah a man. Dad, I am outta here!"

Well, I left home feeling down, wondering did I do the right thing. I can't get the look on my father's face out of my mind. I had hurt my father: my words, my attitude, my actions, yes, I had hurt my father. I heard footsteps behind me. Was that my dad coming after me. I heard a voice say, "Lil dude, what's going on?"

My heart dropped. It was Jack. "Nothing man, my ol' man just put me out. Now I don't have anywhere to go."

Jack replied, "Man, ease up, it ain't all that bad. My ol' man put me out too. Hey, he called me a good-for-nothing, he said I had to learn some things the hard way. What does he know? Hey, did your ol' man tell you that too?

"No, my dad told me he loves me,"

"Well, Lil dude, it's all the same. Ain't no difference from your ol' man or mine; look at it this way, we are free, free to do our own thing."

Well, I went from house to house trying to survive. Things on the street got rough, real rough. I began to steal food to eat, and people on the streets were after me. The gang and I got into some serious trouble in the neighborhood; the neighbors got together and started a neighborhood watch. The police were looking for us; life on the streets turned into hide and seek; nowhere to run and nowhere to hide. What had I gotten myself into? Man, life was fast. You didn't have time to think, you didn't care who you hurt, you trusted no one, and you had to take care of yourself. You had to learn how to survive on the streets in the midnight hours.

My pops was right. Everyone was hiding from their pain and their hurts on these streets, and they didn't care if they gave you their pain. It was just me and the gang, but it was only a few of us now. Some of the members were in jail, or strung out on drugs, or dead. We became just a name on the streets, just a name. One night Jack got caught with some drugs on him; he had to do some time. Well, Jack always looked after me on the streets. Man, it really got rough. The streets, they care for no one. Yeah, the streets call your name in the darkness of the night. In the streets you think you found your fame. In the streets, in the darkness of the night, the streets call your name.

One day, I ran into my mom and sister; they were coming out of the store. I had one of those signs in my hands that said work for money. Man, my mom looked at me, in her eyes I could see love. I hung my head down low. My mom just put her hand under my chin, lifted my face, and she said, "Son look at me."

I looked into my mom's eyes, and what I saw was love, a mother's love. In my mom's eyes I did not see judgment, I saw love. For a moment in my mind, I went back in time to how it used to be back in the day: her lovely smile, her laughter, her gentle spirit, and her singing praises unto the Lord. Oh, I forgot how it used to be, the peace and joy. I heard my mom saying, "Junior, we are going to pray for you, right here and right now. Junior, it was not by accident that I saw you here today; today we pray to the Father for you."

"Father, keep through your name my son whom you have given me. Father, I ask that you watch over him, and that you bring him back to You, remove the blinders from his eyes, remove the hardness of his heart, unplug his ears, and let him hear you. Father, I ask that you speak into his heart, and Lord when he cries out to You, let him know that you are right here with him, and that he is not alone. Let your love overtake him, and Father bring him to his senses. In the name of Jesus."

As my mom and sister ended their prayer, I felt a release that I cannot explain. I'd felt such a void; there was a void in my heart. It seemed as though I was missing something. My mom looked at me and she said, "Whatever happens from here on out, always remember JESUS LOVES YOU, and He is right here with you. Baby, did you hear me? Jesus loves you, and your mama loves you too."

My mom kissed me gently, hugged me and handed me $20.00. Then she said, "Son, if you are hungry, you can come to the house and eat. If you need to bathe and change clothes, you can come to the house." My mama and sister left, but I noticed that my mom was not crying. As she walked away, I overheard her say to my sister, "He's coming back to the Lord, and it's all in God's timing. It's all in God's timing, baby girl. That's why we pray, not just for Junior, but all the lost ones out here, that's why we pray." I continued to look as they drove down the street, remembering my mama's love, and remembering how she loved Jesus.

I didn't go home, I continued to stay in the streets, but after my mom prayed for me, something was different. It was as though the things I was doing, I was uncomfortable doing. I kept remembering the look in my mom's eyes, the look, that look of love. It was powerful, a powerful look, like she knew something, but what did she know?

Things began to get hard, man it was rough in the streets, no longer an adventure. Now it became *watch yourself.* One night, hanging out, someone shot at me. They thought I owed them some money, and they wanted their money. This dude was standing right in from of me; he pulled out his gun, and said, "I want my money, and I want it now."

As he was about to pull the trigger, he had his hand on the trigger, just then in my mind, I heard a voice say, "Move over," and at that moment I moved over, and the bullet went right past my ear. If I had not moved, I would be dead, dead right now. I then remembered the prayer my mama prayed over me and what she said. "Whatever happens from here on out, remember, "JESUS LOVES YOU." Just then, the police pulled up, and they took us in. I got arrested, and I had to do some time in jail. My mama always said that God works in mysterious ways--you know she was right. While I was in jail, I ran into Jack. Yeah, you remember Jack the one who I wanted to follow. Well, I followed Jack, right to jail. Jack had always been hard, he was always rebelling. He had some serious problems in his life.

Come to find out, when Jack was younger, his mother had remarried. Jack was living with his stepfather and mother.

Jack always thought his stepdad was being hard on him. Jack's father left his mom in Jack's early age. Jack's father verbally abused him and his mother. The only thing he remembers is his father leaving and his mother remarrying. In Jack's heart he always wanted his parents to get back together. So, in his eyes, his stepdad was the enemy. What I didn't know is that Jack's stepdad was a minister. Yeah, Jack went to church and he knew about Jesus, but he was angry on the inside. He felt betrayed because his father left, so Jack's heart was hardened; he didn't want any part of his stepfather.

What happened next blew my mind, it just blew me away. I was sitting by myself one night reading the Bible. Yeah, I was reading the Bible, and I could never lose the thought of what my mama said, "...no matter what happens, here on out Jesus loves you." Man that stuck with me. Jesus loves me, me after everything I had done, all the trouble I caused, all the hurt and pain I caused my father, mother, brothers, and sisters, all the pain I caused to come upon other people, all the wrong that I did in the darkness of the night. Me, Jesus loved me--with all the stealing, the using of drugs, the deception, the lies, all the pain I caused. Me, Jesus loves me?

As I pondered on that thought, someone tapped me on my shoulder. I looked up, and it was Jack, yeah, good ol' Jack. Jack stood there looking at me like he did back in the day.

"Lil dude, man." Jack just stood there and as I looked him up and down, he was saying, "Lil dude, I can't believe it's you. " You see, the room I was in reading my Bible, was the room where the outside outreach ministers came. I just couldn't get the thought out of my mind that Jesus loves me. The room started to fill up.

Jack said, "Talk to you later, Lil dude." As the preacher began to open the session with prayer, someone said, "Let's bow our heads and close our eyes." I heard a voice, a familiar voice, saying, "Father, in the name of Jesus..." My mind drifted, that voice, it was so familiar, naw, it can't be, I had to lift my head and open my eyes. *My God,* I heard myself say, *that, that's Jack praying.* I couldn't believe what I was seeing or what I was hearing. Jack, was that Jack? I looked at Jack as he finished the prayer by saying, "Amen." I looked at Jack, and he looked at me, as he stood in the front of everyone in his suit, a sharp suit at that. Look at Jack--Jack was a preacher man!

Jack began by telling the story, our story, that's how I found out about his stepdad, Jack continued, "At one time, I was here, right here in this place, let me tell you what turned my life around. One day I was out on the streets, thinking about what I could get into and two ladies approached me. They were not afraid of the hard look on my face; I did not scare them. One of the ladies asked me if my name was Jack, because I looked familiar. I answered her with an as-a-matter-of-fact and very disrespectful, "Yeah, my name is Jack, what's it to you?" She began, "Jack, I know you and your family. I have been sent to pray for you," As Jack was telling the story he said, "The woman began to pray 'Father, keep through your name Jack, who you have led me to." As he was speaking, my mind raced back to the prayer my mother prayed over me. Jack continued, "Yes, and as she finished the prayer she said, "Jesus loves you, and no matter what happens after this, always remember Jesus loves you."

I could never get that thought out of my heart that Jesus loves me? Jack looked at me and he said, "Your mother and sister prayed for me. When she looked at me, she did not judge me, when she looked at me, I seen love in her heart. Lil dude, your mom and sister prayed for both of us with that same prayer."

She told me, "God has a plan for your life." In spite of everything I'd been through, she said that God was going to use me. Jack concluded the story of how the two women approached him to tell him that Jesus loved him, and how it stayed with him. When he got to jail, he decided to give his life over to the Lord. He decided to live for the Lord. Jack finished, "What you see in front of you is a man who loves the Lord. I am not ashamed to preach the Gospel of Jesus Christ, and to tell you as someone told me, "Jesus loves you."

That night, many prisoners, including some officers, came to give their hearts to the Lord. Yes, yes, even I gave my life to the Lord that night.

Lil dude went on to say, "My beautiful bride, if you agree, could Jack be the minister for our wedding. Jack loves the Lord with all of his heart. He is preaching the Gospel, and he's letting others know about the love of Jesus Christ. I want you to know that I am not perfect, but I do love you. I value you and I respect you. Because of the humility I've been through, the pain, and hurt I've been through, because of all that I've been through, I am able to say, 'I love you.' My parents loved me at my worst, and I have seen Christ in them. I want you to know that I love you. I pray that Jesus will use me to love you the way He has commanded, and that I can be the husband that Jesus has called me to be. I love you."

This is the story of two boys who were raised differently. Both made mistakes and caused a lot of people pain, but one day their lives were changed because someone prayed for them and left the message: "Jesus loves you." As God used two women to pray, the gospel continues on today. By those two women praying over two young men, they received Jesus Christ into their hearts and were set free.

Jesus gave to each and every one of us His all. He has taught us by example through humility, pain and hurt. Jesus Christ has loved us. While He was still on the Cross, His love was so unconditional that He prayed for us. While he was suffering, Jesus Christ took our pain, our sickness, our burdens and they were nailed to the cross. He did not judge us. In his awesomeness He asked the Father to forgive, while He was on the Cross. That is love. That is the "Power of love."

How about you?

Are you experiencing for yourself Jesus' love for you, His unconditional love? Jesus loves you just the way you are. Someone reading this might be going through a personal struggle, you might be feeling unloved, insecure, feeling worthless, or have feelings of low self-esteem or feeling depressed.

Jesus' love is real. He looks at you and He sees your pain, you hurts, your disappointments, frustrations, and your inner struggles. Jesus knows what you are going through.

Just as Jack and Lil dude were at the end of their rope, they did things and saw things. They stole, used drugs, lived on the streets, and they thought the streets were their friend. At the loneliest point in their lives, they accepted Jesus Christ as their Lord and Savior.

There could be a Jack or Lil dude in your family. Won't you tell them that there is someone who loves them unconditionally, just as they are--someone who does not judge them, someone who knows their pain. Won't you tell them about Jesus? Won't you tell them that Jesus loves them and Jesus loves you too!

Annie

"No, no," Annie pleaded. You could hear her scream miles away. Her frail body became motionless; her body appeared as though she was going into shock. The crowd around her was laughing and making jokes about her. Their senseless cruel acts, their cold hearts, and uncompassionate demeanor were obvious. They could care less how Annie was feeling. They yelled out all the more, "Shut up." Annie continued to struggle, she continued to fight, and she tried to hold on with every breath in her body. Annie was not getting weak; she was getting stronger.

She held on, not giving up. She held in her arms what gave her strength, what gave her joy. She was not about to let that go, no matter what she had to endure. She screamed, "Please, don't, please, I beg you, don't," as she continued to plead for what was hers. Her life. "I'll do anything, but please, please don't."

She was struck on her cheek; the blood ran from her mouth. She felt no pain, she continued, "I beg you, please."

You could hear the crowd on the right side of her say, "Quiet her down," and on the left side of her, you could see their tear-stained faces. You could hear their weeping. You could see the pain on their faces. A small group was praying. The crowd was getting louder and louder. You saw Annie kneeling on a small platform, as she continued to plead.

Suddenly, her blouse was torn from off her and the lashes began, but she still held on to the life in her hands. She wouldn't let go. Annie, tears streaming down her face, did not feel the lashes. She continued to cry, "Please, please, please don't, don't take my baby, don't take my baby from me."

The laughter was getting louder and louder. Annie's son was torn from her loving arms. Hysterical, blood running off her back, she pleaded for her baby boy's life, and she pleaded not to be separated from her son. She was willing to do anything to keep her son. But, now he was taken from her.

Her screams were heard miles away, and you could feel her pain. The lashes stopped. Annie felt no pain from the beating. Her pain was the pain from her master selling her son--her only son. Her master looked at her with hatred in his eyes. He kicked her off the selling block platform. Annie felt nothing. Everything she loved had been taken from her, just as she was taken from her mama, from her mama's arms. Annie's son was six years old; but he was her baby boy, he was everything to her. He was her world, her love. Annie did her best to protect her son. The master was in debt, and he needed to pay off some of his bills to get out of debt. So he sold some of his slaves, and Annie's boy was one of them.

His new master took him. You could hear Annie's baby boy screams, "Mama, mama, mama," he shouted loudly with his small voice. "Mama, mama," he was kicking and fighting with all of his little might, crying mama, mama, not knowing what was going on. His new master slapped him across the face and shouted, "You don't have a mama," and he put Annie's baby boy in the wagon with the other newly bought slaves and began to drive away.

Annie, beaten down, was struggling to get to her feet, crying for her son. The wagon you could see from a distance, with the dust billowing in back. Annie on her knees, tears streaming down her cheeks, with the back of her brown skin cut open, and blood oozing out. The crowds began to disperse. Annie's heart was pounding, she felt no pain from the beating--her pain, her pain came from having her love, her baby boy torn from her arms. Annie's heart was broken and her heart was wounded deep within her. Annie still lay on the ground, her frail, limp, bloodied body, and her face to the ground; she whispered with a soft voice, almost mumbling. Through Annie's pain, her heartfelt pain, through her sweat, through her blood, through her tears, Annie softly whispered, *"Nobody knows the trouble I seen, nobody knows my sorrow, nobody knows the trouble I see."*

We all go through things in life and we talk ourselves into believing that nobody cares about us or what we are going through. Nobody knows our trouble or knows our sorrow. That might be almost true with one exception, Jesus knows. He knows what you are going through, your hurt, pain, and sorrow. He knows.

Be merciful to me, O God, for man would swallow me up; fighting all day he oppresses me. My enemies would hound me all day, for there are many who fight against me, O Most High (Psalm 56:1-2 NKJV).

Put my tears into Your bottle, Are they not in Your book? Then my enemies will turn back; this I know for God is for me. In the Lord I will praise His word. In God I have put my trust, I will not be afraid. What can man do to me (Psalm 56:8-11 NKJV).

How Deep Is Your Love

"**G**o take yourself a wife of harlotry And children of harlotry. For the land has committed great harlotry by departing from the Lord. So he went and took Gomer the daughter of Diblaim, and she conceived and bore him a son" (Hosea 1:2, NKJV).

"Let her put away her harlotries from her sight. She will chase her lovers but not overtake them; Yes, she will seek them but not find them" (Hosea 2:2, 7, NKJV).

Not too long ago in America City, there lived a young couple. This couple had its ups and downs, just like other couples. Mrs. Joy's happiness depended on her husband. She went into the marriage as half a person, looking for her husband to make her feel good about herself. Mrs. Joy put a lot of pressure on Mr. Joy, but because Mr. Joy was unable to fulfill this role, his wife went looking for love in all the wrong places. Now, Mr. Joy was a hardworking man who loved and cared for his family. Mrs. Joy, unsatisfied in her marriage, felt her husband no longer loved her the way she felt he should.

Mrs. Joy was so unhappy, unsatisfied, and distraught in her marriage that she took to the streets. One day while she was street-walking she ran into one of her friends. Her friend questioned her and asked why she was doing this. After all, she had a husband at home who loved her. Mrs. Joy told her friend to stop asking all these questions, and said, "Leave me alone. I don't need you turning your nose down at me." Her friend told her, "I just want to help you; there's a better way. Your husband loves you." Mrs. Joy said, "Whatever" and walked away.

Now Mrs. Joy had been doing this awhile, and things at home were very unsettling. One day, Mr. Joy was walking around the corner with two of his friends. One of the guys spotted Mr. Joy's wife. "Man, ain't that your wife? Man, how long has she been on the streets, ain't no shame in her game."

Mr. Joy was stunned looking at his wife, who did not see him. "Man, what you gonna do?" The second guy says, "Yeah, just look at her. Man, you should leave her. You don't need nothing like that in your life. She's no good, just look at her."

Mr. Joy began to speak, "I love my wife; she's going through some rough times right about now."

His friends responded, "Man, you are crazy?"

Mrs. Joy looked around and she saw her husband with his friends. She began to talk to herself, "I love him. I don't know why I do the things that I do. The closer he gets the farther I push him away. The more pain I feel, the more I reject him. He's not around half the time anyway. Some days he makes me happy but most days he doesn't."

She turned her head, and went on doing what she was doing. Mr. Joy was having a hard time with this and a harder time with his friends:

"Man, let her go. You don't need her. Let her go, you don't need her in your life." "Man, why don't you divorce her, you don't need that in your life, disrespecting you like that." "Yeah man, you can't have a woman disrespecting you like that, where is your pride? Here man, here's my phone book, just call any woman in here."

Mr. Joy spoke loudly, "Look, I don't want your phone book. Yeah, that's my wife, but I know that she is hurting. Yeah, you tell me to forget about her, leave her here, but I can't. I love her."

"Man you are weak; you make a brother look bad."

Mr. Joy said, "No, you know you're wrong; you make yourself look bad. I am a man; I took a vow for better or worse. No, I believe in my vows and I believe in God, and right now my wife needs me. You think that I am weak, no; I am a strong man. Me and my wife, we will make it. Why? Because I am a praying man. You think I am weak; no, I am stronger than both of you together. Take a good look at my wife; I believe in Jesus' promises. I know Jesus loves me and my wife and He wants the best for us. Yeah, my brothers, we are going to make it, we will make it."

Mr. Joy left his friends and walked over to his wife. At the same time a man was approaching her. Mr. Joy sternly told the man "She ain't for sale." Mr. Joy reached out to his wife, and she began to cry. "I am so sorry. I didn't mean to hurt you like this; can you forgive me? I didn't mean to embarrass you or humiliate you. I can only imagine the things your friends said. I know how bad you feel. "Why, why don't you leave me, I don't deserve you or your love."

Mr. Joys said, "Listen, I am your husband; I will care and provide for you. For better or worse, I will stand by my vows. I believe in you and me; we can make it work. Those guys, they aren't my friends; I have only one true friend and His name is Jesus. Jesus loves me and forgives me of my sins, and, because of that, I am able to love you and forgive you. It's not going to be easy; it's going to be hard. It's going to take a lot of hard work on both of our parts." Mr. Joy reached out and took his wife's hand. She began, "I am willing. A long time ago, I gave my heart to the Lord, and I stayed away. I am willing to return to Jesus. I want to come back to Jesus and you. I've felt so worthless, so empty, like I had no hope. I now know that I put so much on you for you to make me happy. I know that only Jesus can make me whole."

Mr. Joy said, "Yeah, Jesus is his name and we will serve the Lord together."

As time went on, Mrs. Joy tried to make it work. She remembered the things that she had said to her husband; but, deep inside, the streets were calling her name. She began to feel restless, and those same hurt feelings of her past began to overtake her. Again, she felt unloved, helpless, worthless, and hopeless. No matter what Mr. Joy did, it wasn't good enough. Those same thoughts kept creeping into her mind. Those same thoughts that no one loved her and no matter what, she wasn't going to be good enough. The depression set in even more, and the restlessness continued. Eventually Mrs. Joy went back to the streets. She didn't know why she went back to the streets, she didn't want to, but something kept pulling her into the path of destruction. She tried to fight it, but she couldn't and, deep inside, she knew the horrible pain that it was going to cause her husband. But she went on anyway, day after day after day.

One day, Mr. Joy received a call--a call from the police

department; they had picked up his wife on prostitution charges. He had to go down to the police station and bail his wife out of jail.

Then the Lord said to me, "Go again, love a woman who is loved by a lover, and is committing adultery, just like the love of the Lord for the children of Israel, who look to other gods and love the raisin cakes of pagans." So I bought her for myself for fifteen shekels of silver and one and one-half homers of barley. And I said to her, "You shall stay with me many days, you shall not play the harlot, nor shall you have a man, so too, will I be toward you" (Hosea 3:1-2).

Mr. Joy went and reclaimed his unfaithful wife from jail, and paid the money that was needed for her to be released. Mr. Joy was a faithful husband, but he felt so disappointed, so empty, and so lonely. When his wife was released from jail, he could not say anything. He was so hurt. He kept playing in his mind over and over again what the Lord told him to do. He didn't understand it. He didn't want to do it, but yet he kept in his heart what the Lord instructed him to do. This was a hard test for Mr. Joy. He wanted no part of Mrs. Joy; he felt as though she had ripped his heart right out of him. He felt empty, crushed, and hopeless. Actually, he felt like he was worth nothing. He had so many questions and very few answers.

He felt like a fool. His family was wondering why, why was he still with his wife, after all the humiliation that she had caused him, all the hurt and pain she brought to him? Behind his back his own family talked about him. They just could not understand his reason for staying with his wife.

But Mr. Joy kept replaying in his mind the instructions that the Lord had given him. He talked with the Lord over and over, and he could not understand it himself. But Mr. Joy was a godly man, and He knew that the Lord had given him specific instructions. No matter how he felt or how he looked to others, he had to be obedient to the Lord, and he was. He held his head up high, and began to work on his marriage again. It wasn't easy for Mr. Joy; don't think it was. He still had his own feelings to deal with.

Over time, Mr. Joy just trusted more and more in the Lord. Mrs. Joy had to deal with the worthlessness and hopelessness that she felt. She had to overcome the pain that she caused her husband. They began to work at their marriage and get the help that they needed. They had a hard road in front of them, but with counseling and working together, they made it.

The love that this man had for his wife--that's how Jesus loves you and me. Hosea's purchase of Gomer symbolizes God's great devotion which moves Him to seek reconciliation even if it means subjecting Himself to humiliation: the humility Jesus went through for us to bring us back to His loving arms.

What about you? Can you learn to love someone like this, like Jesus did? He is our example and we should follow Him. This is symbolized by the way Mr. Joy stood up to his friends and took a firm stand for his wife, his marriage, and the love that he had for his wife. That's love. Even though, his wife went back to the streets, Mr. Joy had to again put his feelings aside and be obedient to the instructions that God had given him. He was devoted to his wife and, in the midst of it all, he showed her mercy.

That's how it is for us; Jesus has showed us mercy and continues to show us mercy. His mercy is new every morning (Lamentations 3:23, NKJV). That's Love.

Facing the Future with Courage

I t was a clear, crisp, cold, Saturday morning, my husband and I decided to go to Washington D.C. and see the
"Memorial Wall." As we got out of our car the wind blew
around us. We zipped and buttoned our coats, pulled up our
coat collars, put on our warm winter gloves, caps over our
heads, and we proceeded on our journey. A journey I will
never forget.

As we walked, we came upon three bronze statues of three
soldiers; these soldiers were all dressed in their military gear,
with their weapons in their hands and on their backs. It would
appear that these three soldiers shared an experience, and you
could sense the closeness about them. This was the entrance
to the "Memorial Wall."

As we came upon the "Memorial Wall," the people all
around me had a solemn look on their faces. As I looked at my
husband's expression; it seemed as if he was a million miles
away. He was feeling and sensing emotions with which I was
unfamiliar. The look in his eyes was as if he was remembering

all that he had been through—as if he was reliving the pain, the torment, and all the confusion that was around him at that time. As if he was remembering all of those that died around him and beside him. The "Memorial Wall" was in front of us with so many names. Families were looking for the names of their loved ones, their eyes going up and down, back and forth searching the "Memorial Wall" for their loved one's name. Families were holding on to each other, and you could hear the deafening silence in the air and feel the wind blowing by.

The "Memorial Wall" is 246.75 feet long and the height 12 ft.10 inches. The material is granite, and holds 58,209 names. Each panel holds approximately 144 lines, and the names are in chronological order by the date they were taken. As we continued to look at each panel, and to touch the names of those on the "Memorial Wall," I noticed there were diamonds by some names and crosses by other names. If a name had a cross by it they were still missing, and if a name had a diamond by it they were accounted for. As I looked at all of the poems, flowers, and pictures of soldiers on different panels of the "Memorial Wall, I can sense that this was the beginning of a healing process for some and for others a closure. As we came to the last panel, with the last name, I looked back to the beginning of the Memorial Wall--at all the people searching for names, touching the panel of names, and I remembered, as we first began our journey, and saw the three soldiers thinking of the experience that the Vietnam Soldiers shared. I saw the families reflecting on the shared experience of the Vietnam Veterans and the Vietnam War. As we started to leave the Memorial Wall, we pulled up our collars, put on our warm winter gloves, and said goodbye to the names of many.

The air was still crisp, but not as cold, as we continued on our journey. We came to the Lincoln Memorial, and my soul was stirred with excitement. So much went on here at the Lincoln Memorial. We walked up the stairs, the stairs where so many before us had walked. We went inside to the huge Memorial of Lincoln, which is 19 feet tall and 19 feet wide. On the north side of the wall is Lincoln's Gettysburg address and on the south side of the wall is Lincoln's second Inaugural address. As I look at the words from his Gettysburg address, I am amazed, because coming from the Memorial Wall, this speech seemed as if it was for today. A part of the speech states: "The brave men living and dead who struggle here have consecrated it far above our poor power to add or detract. The world will little note nor long remember what we say here but it can never forget what they did here. It is for us the living rather to be dedicated here to the unfinished work. That we here highly resolve that these dead shall not have died in vain." Awesome!

Here I was, standing on the steps where Martin Luther King Jr. gave his famous renowned speech, "I have a Dream." I looked in front of me as far as to the Washington Monument, and for the first time I saw what many before me have experienced. As I continued to just look around me and take everything in, I saw people looking in the direction that I was looking in. But, you see, they did not see what I saw; they did not feel what I was feeling. I saw the community coming together for a cause. I saw the people all around this Memorial standing and listening to the great speech. No, they could not imagine what I was sensing, no, they could not imagine what I was feeling. I saw for the first time how many before me struggled to get to where I am standing. They came in buses, trucks, cars, and on foot. They struggled to get to Washington D.C. to hear a great speech. Not knowing how great the speech would be that day and on to this day, and not knowing the impact that it still holds. They came together in numbers, they were unified. They were tired of what was going on. They wanted answers; they wanted solutions to the problems. Yes, I can see that they came in great record numbers.

As I looked around I could remember at the age of seven, when I heard King give his speech. I remember, because my parents were watching it on TV, and how intensely they were listening to the speech. All around me, all the way to the Washington Monument, I could see people. I continuously say the Washington Monument because this was a great distance from the Lincoln Memorial from where I was standing. I could see the impact that this had on Washington D.C. All of America had to look that day at the unity of the people coming together, who came together for a cause, and they came together in great numbers.

Yes, the people around me could not imagine what I saw, for they could not see what I saw. They only saw what was in front of them, but I could see our past, present, and future. I saw great things. I saw all the people who struggled before me and who paved the way for me. The people who marched on Washington wanted a better future for people like you and me. They were beaten, dog-bitten, sprayed with water hoses, thrown in jail, hospitalized, and yes, even killed so that I could be where I was today.

We each have a responsibility, as the people did who went before us. My mother was a nurse, and she sweated and shed some tears to graduate from her class and become a nurse. Was it easy? No, but she paved the way for my sister and myself, and not just for us, but also for many who have the privilege of being nurses today. My father was a truck driver. I've seen for myself how hard he had to work for my mom, my sister, and myself. Was it easy? No, he struggled and he had to pave the way. My husband was an officer in the Army; he paved the way for his sons, and not only them, but for others who have come up in the ranks.

We, as individuals, should not become complacent regarding where we are; we have to pave the way for others that are behind us. We should encourage and help other people. We should help build people up: the young, the middle-aged, and the seniors. We do not know the impact that we may have on someone's life. We have a responsibility to our children, our children's children, and other's children.

As Martin Luther King said, "I have a dream." So each of us should have a dream.

As our day came to an end, we walked down the steps, overwhelmed at all that happened here on August 28, 1963. Pulling up our collars and putting on our warm winter gloves, it appeared to us as though it was not as cold now. Yes, the air was still crisp but I hardly noticed.

This was an awesome experience for me, one that I pray I will never forget. You see, I have walked down the steps that Martin Luther King walked down and I stood on the steps where Miriam Anderson sang to millions. I clearly see for the first time what the march on Washington was all about. Did I have to go to Washington to find this out? No. But the Lord allowed me to see what so many before me have seen. Do we have a responsibility to our young people and all people as well? Yes. We have to pass on our dreams and allow others to dream their dreams.

I've seen the past and where we came from, and I know that in our present we must move forward. We cannot become complacent, and the struggle for today is not just for today but for the future.

The Homecoming

"Then He said: 'A certain man had two sons. And the younger of them said to his father, "Father, give me the portion of good that falls to me"' (Luke 15:11, NKJV).

"So he divided to them his livelihood. And not many days after, the younger son gathered all together, journeyed to a far country, and there wasted his possessions with prodigal living. But when he had spent all, there arose a severe famine in that land and he began to be in want. Then he went and joined himself to a citizen of that country, and he sent him into the fields to feed swine. And he would gladly fill his stomach with the pods that the swine ate, and no one gave him anything.

"But when he came to himself, he said, 'How many of my father's hired servants have bread enough and to spare, and I perish with hunger. I will arise and go to my father, and will say to him, "Father, I have sinned against heaven and before you, and I am no longer worthy to be called your son. Make me like one of your hired servants.'

"And he arose and came to his father. But when he was

still a great way off, his father saw him and had compassion, and ran and fell on his neck and kissed him. And the son said to him, 'Father, I have sinned against heaven and in your sight, and am no longer worthy to be called your son.'

"But the father said to his servants, 'Bring out the best robe and put it on him and put a ring on his hand and sandals on his feet. And bring the fatted calf here and kill it, and let us eat and be merry for this my son was dead and is alive again; he was lost and is found.' And they began to be merry.

"Now his older son was in the field. And as he came and drew near to the house, he heard music and dancing. So he called one of the servants and asked what these things meant. And he said to him, 'Your brother has come, and because he has received him safe and sound, your father has killed the fatted calf.'

"But he was angry and would not go in. Therefore his father came out and pleaded with him. So he answered and said to his father, 'Lo, these many years I have been serving you; I never transgressed your commandment at any time; and yet you never gave me a young goat that I might make merry with my friends. But as soon as this son of your came, who has devoured your livelihood with harlots, you killed the fatted calf for him.'

"And he said to him, 'Son, you are always with me, and all that I have is yours. It was right that we should make merry and be glad, for your brother was dead and is alive again, and was lost and is found'" (Luke 15: -32, NKJV).

As she stood there clinging onto her husband, with tears streaming down her cheeks, you could hear the anguish in her cry, as she cried out, "Why, why, oh why, did he have to run away? Why did he have to leave home? Doesn't he know how much we love him? Why did he do this? Why did he run away?"

Julius gently lifted up his wife's face, and wiped away her tears, and, speaking in a calm voice, he said, "It's going to be alright. Stop crying, it will be ok."

Debbie was clinging onto her husband, weeping painfully. Julius continued: "It's going to be alright. God didn't bring us this far to leave us." He then looked over to his youngest son, Mark, speaking with pain but trying to be strong at the same time. He said, "I have to go to work, watch over your mother for me." Julius tenderly kissed Debbie on her cheeks and left.

Mark asked his mom, "If you will be alright, I have to go to soccer practice. Can I get you anything?" Debbie, looked at her youngest son. She reached out for him, hugging him in her arms. With tears slowly dripping down her cheeks, she said, "No, you go on ahead, I will be just fine, really, I will be fine."

"O.K., I love you, Mom." As Mark left the house and locked the door behind him. Debbie was left alone in her room, she began to sob uncontrollably, saying, "Lord, watch over my son, let no hurt or harm come to him and protect him. Oh God, all this pain, oh, the pain. Lord, I know you are going to bring me out of this. I need your strength and I need to feel your presence. Oh, God, the pain, the pain."

The following day we find Julius cutting wood for the fireplace. As Julius chopped the wood, he was talking to himself. "I tried to be a good father. I tried to be an example for my sons, and I tried to show him what it is like being a man--the hard knocks and punches that a man has to take. I worked so he could see that a man works, protects, and provides for his family. Yes, I disciplined him; I was hard on him. That's how you learn. I wonder if I was too hard on him. I was a good father. Lord, watch over my son."

Mark, sitting in his room, asked himself, "Why did my brother have to run away? What was he thinking about? He didn't seem to know how bad he made Mom and Dad feel or me. He ran out on me too. He's my big brother and I need him. Man, this is all messed up. God, watch over my brother."

Samantha, the baby sister, was at a youth retreat when all of this happened. We found her on her bed in her bedroom, crying softly and holding on to her favorite bear. "I don't believe this is happening to our family. I can't believe that my brother just took off. He didn't say a word, he just left. I don't believe it." Crying softly, with tears dripping down on her pillow, she whispered, "Oh, I am going to miss him. We, we, were able to talk about anything. He would tell me what guys to stay away from. He always looked after me. Oh God, watch over my brother."

As time goes by, Debbie still felt her pain, her emptiness. "Lord, I don't know what's going on. I don't know why all of this is happening. My son, my baby, he's gone. Lord, I don't know where he is at or what he is doing. I don't understand, I tried to be a good mother, a godly mother. I talked to my kids; I listened to my kids, but what's going on? Her head hung down, tears streaming down her cheeks, and still the pain in her voice, "Lord, my family is hurting right about now." She lifted her head toward heaven, sobbing, "Lord, we need you. Lord, I won't complain or murmur. I know that you watch over all of us. Watch over my son, Lord. I have to be strong; I have to keep on keeping on. Lord, Father, help me get over the pain."

Outside on the family patio, Samantha and Mark were sitting and talking at the table. Mark said, "Mom and dad, they are really taking this hard.

"Yeah, we are too, we're hurting. How could he do this to our family?" Samantha said. "He thinks it's easy out there, doing his own thing, not having any rules to follow. He was only thinking about himself."

Mark nodded. "Yeah, he doesn't care about us; he only cares about himself. I hate to see Mom cry, I've never seen her cry like that."

Samantha said," I know; that's a mother's love. That's how deep they love, and Dad is working harder and later. He tries to keep busy to keep his mind off the problem."

"Lil sis, how do you feel?"

Samantha replied, "I'm hurt and sad. He's the oldest kid; he's always been there for me-- there for both of us. Mark, how do you feel?"

"I don't know, I'm sad he's gone. I miss him. I always looked up to him. You know, I think I am angry, yes, I am angry. How could he run off on us? You know, that's what he did, he didn't just leave Mom and Dad. He left us too." Mark and Samantha hugged each other, and as they did, they caught a glimpse of their mother outside standing by the weeping willow tree.

Debbie is talking to her heavenly Father, "Father, you see where I cannot see; you go where I cannot go. One thing I know for sure is that you care for my son as much as I do. He's yours Father, sealed in the precious blood of Jesus. Father, watch over him. I won't complain. I am trusting in you; this is the hardest test ever. But I am trusting in you to bring me through."

GOING ON......

Julius, Debbie and the kids tried to put their lives back together, tried going on with their daily routines. They tried to be strong. Julius was working hard. Debbie was praying even more; she knew that God hears and answers prayers. Samantha was studying harder, bringing in excellent grades, and Mark was made Captain of the track and football teams. The family continued to pray for their son and brother. Occasionally you would see someone going into or coming out of his room.

You see, it was not easy on the family. What one family member did had an effect on the whole family. Samantha looked at her oldest brother as her protector. Mark was angry and felt like his brother ran out on him. Julius and Debbie at one point were questioning themselves about how they were raising their son. A lot of what-if's came to the surface. But in the family's difficult moments, they drew closer to each other and closer to God.

We don't know why God allows pain in our lives or why He chooses the methods that He does. What we do know is that God is the potter and we are the clay, God molds and shapes us. There will come a time in our lives when we will trustingly and willingly have to rely on Him.

The family was in the family room with the exception of Mark, who was at practice. The phone rang and Julius answered the phone. He heard a "click" at the other end. He said to Debbie, "One of those kids friends calling here and hanging up." He returned to reading his Bible, while Debbie and Samantha talked. The phone rang again, and this time Debbie answered the phone. "Hello, hello. Well, if you don't say anything I am going to hang up." There was a pause, then with a scared voice she heard, "Mom?" Debbie quickly jumped to her feet and said loudly, "Son, son is this you, baby?"

"Yeah Mom, it's me."

Debbie began waving her hands in the air, "My baby is on the phone," she said excitedly. "Where are you, how are you? Are you alright? When are you coming home?" Crying and smiling, she gave the phone to Julius. She was weeping uncontrollably, and she began to thank God. As Julius held the phone in his hand, with trembling hands, he put the receiver to his ear, and with nervousness in his voice he said, "Son, where are you?"

The oldest son, Jimmie, began, "Dad, I know I messed up. Dad, I know I messed up bad."

"Son, where are you, are you alright?'

Jimmie spoke with a humbled voice, with quivering lips, and his eyes welling up with tears, "I know I hurt you and Mom. I know I hurt the family, but Dad it wasn't what I thought it would be. I thought I was going to party and have some really good times, come and go as I pleased, not have to listen to anyone, but it wasn't like that. I found out that I didn't have anywhere to go. You know, I've seen things that I've never seen before. I've been places where you can't imagine. Dad, these streets, the darkness of the night--I thought that's what I wanted. I was wrong, so very wrong. Dad, when my money ran out, I found I had no friends; I've been hungry with no money and no change of clothing, nowhere to lay my head. These streets are dangerous. I've been sleeping in bus stations, in parks, homeless shelters, in doorways, and in the back of alleys. I've been cold, beaten, and left feeling like there was no hope.

"Dad, when I--when I, woke up this morning, I came to myself. I said, "I will ask my father if I can come home. When I came to myself, I said, 'I will ask my father: can I come home, so I can see you and mom, so I can enjoy my mother's cooking again, and can see my sister and brother?' Now I know, Dad, that I can follow your rules. You see, Dad, I've learned from the streets that this isn't where I want to be. Everything happens in the darkness, the blackness of the night. I want to come home and act like your son. I know I made some terrible mistakes and caused a lot of pain, and I am so sorry, but Dad, may I come home?"

Julius spoke with tears in his eyes and big tears running off his face (Oh, the love of a father). "Son, where are you?"

"Dad, I'm right across the street at the payphone. I've been traveling four to five days trying to get home. I don't look good or smell good. I'm at the lowest point in my life and I don't know what to do, except to come home. You could hear the brokenness, the helplessness, the humility in his voice and cry. Julius said, "Son, I don't care what you look like or what you smell like. You come on home, come on home."

In the background you could hear Debbie, "My baby, my son, he's coming back home. Thank you, Jesus, thank you, Lord, thank you, Father; I know the prayers of the righteous availed much. God hears our prayers. We just have to sincerely trust in him. Thank you, Jesus."

As Jimmie was approaching the porch in his dirty clothes and messy hair, you could see the tears pouring down his face. As he walked onto the porch, you saw a broken young man. Julius grabbed his son, and father and son, they both cried together. Julius began to speak happily, "Come on in, son, we are going to celebrate your homecoming. You can have your room back, you can come out of those clothes. Your clothes are still in your closet. Glad you are home, son, glad you're home." Debbie, crying, reached out her hands and her hands were trembling. Jimmie grabbed his mother's hands and said, "Mama, I missed you," and both cried together. The son whispered into his mother's ear, "There's nothing like a mother's love." Samantha joined them, and all four cried together. They were shedding tears of joy, hugging, kissing, kissing, and hugging each other. Tears of joy for an answered prayer; God answers prayers in His time.

As Mark entered the house, he heard all this noise, and said, "What's going on? I hear all this noise, is everyone... he stopped in the middle of his sentence. He saw Jimmie, his oldest brother, and a flood of mixed emotions overtook him. Julius said, "Your brother is back, and we are going to celebrate." Both brothers looked at each other, tears began to flow, Jimmie began, "I missed you, man," and Mark said," I missed you too." They both embraced (there's nothing like a brother's love).

This is what happens in a family, what one person does has an effect on the whole family. It affects each person differently. We think that when we do something it is only affecting us. We need to realize that in the family everyone is affected.

In this story you've learned how a family loves and forgives. That's how Jesus loves us. He loves us unconditionally. He forgives us and accepts us as we are. The love that surpasses all love is the love of Jesus. Jesus loves you and accepts you as you are.

This story was about a man who had two sons, and the youngest son asked his father for his inheritance and then left home. While he was in the world he found out how cruel the world can be. He finally came to himself and returned home, hoping his father would accept him back.

Delilah's Story

D elilah was a beautiful young lady, with big brown eye, and red shoulder-length hair. She wore a smile daily, and when she smiled you could see the deep dimples in her cheeks. If you needed help, Delilah was the girl to call. She carried herself the way her grandmother raised her, to have pride in who she was, take pride in what she did, and to always put God first.

Delilah was thirty-one years old, graduated from one of the most prestigious colleges as a doctor, and was about to begin her internship. This is Delilah's story …

It was a beautiful day, and Delilah was elated as she leaped out of bed, because this was the day she was to begin her medical internship at the hospital. She dashed into the bathroom and an hour later she was putting on the finishing touches of her make-up and pulling her red wavy hair back into a French roll. A half hour later she walked into the hospital, and she heard someone say, "Good morning, Dr. Caldwell." She smiled and nodded her head. She was thinking, " I made it, I have it all: a nice apartment with beautiful furniture, I drive a convertible red BMW, bills paid, and on top of all that, I even look good."

Her first day as an intern went well; she began to meet doctors, nurses and other staff members. Everyone quickly took to Delilah Caldwell. About two weeks later Dr. Caldwell received a phone call. A phone call from her past, a past she wanted to forget. Delilah heard a strong voice, the voice she wanted to forget, the voice she tried to forget: "Hey, babe."

Delilah stuttered, "Hi, how did you find me?"

On the other end of the phone, the voice said, "Oh, you sound surprised. You know I was never going to let you go. You know, I've been thinking about you, and I really miss you." Delilah began to forget everything she went through, his voice made her feel weak, just the sound of his voice made her weak. Delilah heard herself say, "A.J. where are you?"

A.J. replies, "I'm at the airport. I should be at your place in about an hour."

Delilah said, "A.J. wait, but we are over with--we're through."

"Babe, my sweet Delilah, you know how I feel about you. I made a mistake, but I want to make it up to you. You know how I feel about you, girl. I'm going to be everything to you. See you in about an hour."

Delilah heard a click; she stood there with the phone in her hand with mixed emotions. She never really got over A.J. or got him out of her system. She still loved A.J. After everything that she went through, everything that he took her through, A.J. still had a hold on her. She ran home and jumped into the shower, and put on her favorite dress that revealed her shape.

She let her hair down so it could fall gently on her shoulder, and in her heart she was melting. Her mind was telling her no, no, don't forget what he did to you--don't forget. The doorbell rang, Delilah jumped up and looked into the mirror one last time. She put on her favorite perfume and ran to the door. Once she reached the door her mind told her, *You haven't seen him in over a year, remember it's all over, remember what he did, don't fall for the same game, don't fall for the hype, don't open the door.* She put her hand on the lock, unlocked the door, and she slowly opened it.

A.J. stood there in his black leather pants, black turtleneck sweater, and his black leather jacket. A.J. was 6'1" with medium complexion, green eyes, and a slim muscular build. He smiled at Delilah and her heart dropped into her stomach, her palms were sweaty and her knees were weak. A.J. stood there with his Louie Vuitton luggage in his hand, and the so-sure smile on his face, and he seductively called Delilah's name. Her heart was pounding fast; she finally said "Come in."

A.J. put his luggage down, looked at Delilah and said, "I was a fool for letting you go. I was wrong for the things that I did. Girl, I need you in my life, you make me complete. Without you there isn't no me. You and me, we belong together. Delilah, baby, you and me, you and me together, rocking each other's world." A flood of mixed emotions came over Delilah; she still loved that man. The only thing she saw was a fine man in front of her, her man. In her heart she believed she could take a second chance, but in her mind the warning signs were blasting: No, no, no, don't believe him, don't believe the hype.

Delilah stammered, "You know A.J. you really hurt me,

you lied to me, you deceived me, you used me, and you abused me. I can't go back to the way it was. I have to move forward--forward without you A.J. I am doing fine by myself." A.J. gingerly put his hand under Delilah's face and began. "Delilah, I promise you I have changed, just give me another chance. Let me prove my love to you, let me show you girl that can't nobody take your place. Nobody can rock my world like you, nobody, girl. Please give me another chance."

Now, Delilah was like butter in A.J.'s hand, and he knew it; he could see her weakening. He now had to put it on thick, he had to win her over, he had to come on strong, but not too strong. He let a tear drop and shouted out, "Girl, I love you, you hear me? I love you, I can't live without you. I want to be here with you. I can't make it without you, and you're the only one who understands me."

He grabbed her hands. Delilah was having a tremendous fight within herself; she wanted desperately to believe that he had changed. A.J. began to wipe away the tears from her eyes. He grabbed her, held her tight in his arms, and gently kissed her. The next morning, Delilah was awakened with orange juice, coffee, scrambled eggs, sausage, toast, and a long red stemmed rose.

A.J. began, "You and me, babe, me and you." He continued, "I will drive you to work so I can find a job. Girl, I am going to take care of you. I am going to show you that I have changed."

As Delilah got out of her car and went into the hospital, she was floating on cloud nine. She said to herself, "I know that A.J. has changed; this time it's going to be better. This time it's going to work."

A.J. went back to the apartment and relaxed. Sitting back on the couch, he smiled to himself. Things went well for A.J. and Delilah. She continued to work, and A.J. continued to look for a job. He continued to feed on Delilah's weakness. After a while, A.J. felt that he was in; he had Delilah's heart, and all of her love.

Delilah was preparing for work one morning, and she put her shoulder length hair into a French roll as usual. A.J. said, "Don't you get tired of that same old hair style? Girl, you need to do something. That hairstyle makes you look old, and that lipstick—you need to change that too."

Shocked, Delilah looked at A.J., "But A.J., I thought you liked it. I thought you liked my lipstick and hair like this."

A.J. quickly replied, "Oh, baby, you know I do. I just want you to look a little better. You want me to tell you how I feel now, don't you?"

"Yeah, A.J. I want to know. I want to please you." A.J. grabbed Delilah playfully. "Girl-you know I love you, now don't you?"

Over the weeks the verbal abuse continued, and A.J. grew harsher and harsher with his words to Delilah.

Delilah, the young woman who was so sure of herself, began to doubt herself. She now wanted to please A.J. and she began to lose herself. A.J. still had not found a job. One evening, A.J. did not pick Delilah up from work, and she had to take a cab home. It was hours before A.J. showed up at the apartment with liquor on his breath. Delilah began, "Where have you been? I waited an hour for you to pick me up and you never showed up, I had to take a cab home. Where were you?"

A.J. calmly replied, "I was with the fellas and the time went by. Hey now, just be cool girl, why you acting all crazy?"

Delilah shouted back, "Crazy, acting crazy? You have my car, and you don't pick me up from work."

"Babe, just chill, just chill out." He grabbed her, kissed her and said, "You know, it's just you and me."

More and more it became evident that Delilah was losing herself, losing herself in A.J. One evening A.J. had not made it home yet. Delilah called her grandmother, "Grandma, I just wanted to call and say hi, and see how you are doing?"

Grandma replied, "Sweetie, you sound down; what's wrong?

Delilah said, "Oh, nothing is wrong, I just wanted to hear your voice. I love you, grandma."

"Baby girl, you know that your grandmother loves you, and I am proud of you, and I am praying for my baby girl. Sweetie, you know whenever you want to talk, Grandma is here for you. No matter what time it may be, just call your grandma."

Delilah responded, "Love you, grandma." You see, Delilah was not quite ready to open up to her grandmother and let her know what was going on in her life. But Delilah's grandmother knew that something was not quite right.

That evening Delilah went to bed alone. The next morning there was a meeting at the hospital, and Delilah had to attend the meeting. That morning, she had to take a cab to work. Later that evening, A.J. was on time to pick Delilah up. While he was waiting for her, he saw the doctors coming out of the hospital and he became jealous. As Delilah got into the car, he quickly asked her, "Which one of the doctors are you talking to? And don't lie to me." He continued: "I know you're talking to one of those doctors." They drove home in silence. A.J. broke the silence and quickly shouted, "Oh, now you don't have anything to say?"

Now Delilah was remembering all the pain that she went through with A.J. before. She asked herself, "How could I have fallen so hard again; how could I fallen for all the lies again? How could I have been so stupid?" She caught a tear before it rolled down her cheek. That evening, A.J. took Delilah out to a fine dinner and the movies. He assured her that he loved her, and he just goes crazy sometimes, because he loves her so much, and he doesn't want to lose her. Again, he took her into his arms; and again Delilah melted like butter.

One Saturday morning, Delilah wanted to surprise A.J. so, she went to the hair salon, and she cut her shoulder length hair into a beautiful bob. The hairdresser told her she looked gorgeous; the ladies in the salon told her she looked fabulous. She felt really good about herself and her new hairstyle. She felt like the old Delilah. She went home and put on a beautiful pantsuit, added finishing touches to her make-up and added a few touches to her hair. She couldn't wait to surprise A.J. Finally, A.J. arrived home. Delilah stepped out of the room and called, "Surprise."

A.J. looks at her, and he shouted, "What have you done to yourself? You, you, cut your hair--look at you, that doesn't look good." Delilah stood there in shock, tears rushing down her face and she said, "What? You don't like it? I did this for you. I thought you would like it." A.J. replied, "Well, I don't like it."

Over the next months the insults continued, the verbal abuse continued, and still Delilah had decided that she was going to make A.J. happy. She was going to change for him.

She went out of her way to please her man--her man, A.J.
Meanwhile, A.J. had found a job and he worked off and on just
to quiet Delilah down. Delilah's routine was working and waiting on A.J. to come home. One evening, her girlfriend (whom
she hadn't seen for a while because of A.J.) called her and in-
vited her to dinner. At first, Delilah hesitated, but she decided
to go with her girlfriend. On their way to the restaurant, Delilah
spotted A.J.in her car with another woman. Her friend tried
to comfort her. Delilah's heart was broken. So many questions
were going through her head. She went home brokenhearted.

A.J. finally arrived home, and Delilah lost her cool. She
demanded to know where he was and who he was with. She
told him that she saw him with another woman. A.J. denied it,
and talked himself out of it--talked Delilah into believing him.
While at work, Delilah received a phone call, from the "other
woman." She told Delilah things about A.J. and how Delilah
was standing in their way. Delilah was outraged and, with
mixed emotions, called A.J. onto the carpet, and he denied it
all. Delilah, with her tears and her heart in her hand, called her
grandmother. She told her grandmother everything that she'd
been through. Her grandmother prayed with her, and she told
her granddaughter that she knew what she is going through.

Her grandmother began, "Baby girl, I cannot tell you what
to do. You have to be tired of what you are going through; you
have to know that it's not going to get any better. Sweetie, you
have to think with your mind and not your heart. Baby girl, I
know how you feel. You see when a woman has sex with a man
and loves that man--for the man it's sex, but for the woman it's
much more than that. You are connected, you have bonded.
Baby girl, you see she is tied to that man emotionally, with her

whole being, with her heart, her mind and her soul. She is tied to that man and has given her all to that man. It's hard for her to walk away. She has so many mixed emotions; her heart is telling her one thing and her mind is telling her something else. It's hard for the woman to detach herself from the man. The woman gives herself, her love and her mind to that man. Why? Because they have been made into one. You can walk away from this relationship, but, baby girl, you can't do it in your own strength. However, you can in Christ Jesus. Baby girl, you were raised in church; you know that you have to be equally yoked and let Jesus give you your husband. Yes, you made mistakes, you've been hurt and now your heart is broken. But, baby girl, I am not telling you that you won't hurt, that you won't feel any pain--no, I am not saying that. You can walk away with bitterness for men, or you can give your hurt to the Lord, your pain and your disappointments to God.

"You see, baby girl, I know what you're going through, because I went through the same thing too with your grandfather. Yes, baby girl, I was hurt, yes, I walked around with my heart in my hand. I cried many a river. But, baby girl, I'm not just saying all this just to say it. I want you to know that I feel your pain. I know what it feels like to have to taste your bitter tears. I know that you're hurting; you can't believe that he did that to you. You can't believe that you fell for all the lies. But over time, yes, over time and with time you can get over this. You might have some sleepless nights, but on those nights let Jesus rock you to sleep. You will have long days and long nights, but Jesus will be with you comforting you on those restless days and restless nights. There comes a time in our lives when we have to move on and move forward in Jesus. Baby, you deserve better. You don't need nobody to talk you down, have you confused, and think that don't nobody want you. You are intelligent, beautiful, and you have a bright future ahead of you."

Delilah asked, "Grandma, how did you make it?"

"Baby girl, it was one of the hardest things I've been through. I had to go to Jesus daily asking for His strength and mostly for me to be able to forgive. You see, back in my day it was different, and I believed in God's promises and the promise that He made to me. I had to trust Jesus with my pain, my disappointments, and my unmet expectations. I had to believe God and take Him at His word. God spoke to me and said 'I know the plans I have for you they are plans of good and not evil, plans to give you a future and a hope' (Jeremiah 29:11).

"Baby girl, God wants to give you a future, and He wants to give you hope. Baby girl, you don't have to despair because God gives hope to the hopeless and He gives love to the loveless. You don't have to go through that mess with that man; you have to trust in God."

Delilah asked, "Grandmother, will the pain ever go away?"

"Over time, baby girl, over time, you have to let time run its course. One thing I know for sure, you can make it. Let God guide you and bless you the way He plans to."

Delilah took Grandma's words to heart, but it was not for that time but for an appointed time.

Again Delilah fell and was deceived by A.J., but when she really got tired, she walked away and left A.J. right where he was. Delilah re-gave her heart to the Lord; she trusted Jesus and gave her disappointments to Him. Mostly, she asked God not to let her become bitter, but to let her continue in love. Delilah had a heart and a love for Jesus. She chose for herself to follow Jesus.

I pray that this story of Delilah touched you in a special way. This could be any woman who is confused, or has lost her way. We are not to be judgmental, for we must all carry our own cross. Your cross is not my cross and my cross is not your cross. Let us learn to be there for each other, in love, with a touch, a kind word, and words of encouragement.

There are many women who are like Delilah, or have been like her at one time or another. If you have never walked in Delilah's shoes, then you should praise God right now. Walking in Delilah's shoes is not easy, for, you see, Delilah was so sure about herself. She thought that she had made it, that she had it all. But you see the enemy comes in to kill, steal, and destroy. You may have had an A.J. in your life at one time or another. Or if you know someone that is a Delilah or A.J. then you should pray for them. Pray in their behalf for deliverance and pray that they be set free. Pray that they be able to walk in the things that Jesus has called them to walk in.

Delilah was distraught regarding what she was going through. She had self-esteem, but her self-esteem was taken away, she lost herself and tried to be someone else to please a man. You see, Delilah loved and she loved hard. As women, mothers, aunts, or grandmothers, we should encourage and help any female, no matter what age. We should be able to tell them that, in time, they will be able to love again and laugh again. We should be willing to pray for and encourage a Delilah who may walk across our path.

Joanna

It was a lovely day outside, the sun was shining, the grass was the deepest green, the roses were blooming, the wind was blowing and the birds were singing. You could hear the laughter of children in the distance. The neighbors were out cutting grass, planting flowers, and washing their cars. Oh, the day was simply beautiful.

As I stood in my front yard, watching all that was going on around me, my mind took me back to what happened just a few days ago. It was a normal day, nothing out of the ordinary. The phone rang and, on the second ring, I picked up the phone. "Hello?"

On the other end of the phone, it was my sister, Joanna. She blurted out, "It's Mom, she's in the hospital—we had to rush her to the hospital. You need to get down here now."

"What happened?" I asked. Joanna shouted back, "Girl, just get down here now. We need you--we don't know yet what it is, but it is serious." She hung up the phone abruptly.

Since I didn't live in the same town with my mama and

other family members, it was going to take me eight hours to get to Seattle. When my sister called, it was about 10:00 p.m.. I prayed and asked God to heal my mother. I quoted all the scriptures I knew over and over. I packed a bag for the kids and me. Early the next morning, I was on the road with my kids. My heart was racing fast. I was scared. I didn't know what to expect. Joanna wouldn't tell me anything over the phone. As I was driving to the hospital, I had all these questions in my mind and no answers.

I told the kids we were going to Seattle to see Grandma because she was in the hospital. I tried to explain everything to them without sounding fearful. I was praying and praying hard. This was Mama that was sick, this was my mama. It felt as though it was taking me forever to get to Seattle. I couldn't get there fast enough.

I prayed, "Lord, don't take my mama, let me see my mama." Mama had taken ill a couple of days earlier, my sister had taken her to the doctor and the doctor said that mama had pneumonia. They wanted to put her in the hospital then, but, being strong-willed, she talked the doctor out of it. He had Mama sign a release stating that he tried to get her to go to the hospital but she refused. Mama wouldn't listen to anyone; she had made up her mind, and she wasn't going to any hospital. I called Joanna while I was on the road and she said it didn't look good. That's all she would say. Joanna liked to be in control, she always tried to control everybody. She was one of those people who had no control over her own life, so she always tried to control others.

I thought about Joanna for a moment and felt sorry for her. Joanna had been married three times and she had four kids. Let me try to explain Joanna to you so you will soon see why she always tries to control someone else. Joanna married her first husband, Tom, when she was young because she got pregnant. My daddy sat Tom down and explained to him why he was going to marry his daughter, Joanna. You see my daddy was a respectful man who had plenty. He was looked up to in the community, and no one was going to embarrass his family in any way. By the time my daddy got through talking to Tom, he was ready to marry Joanna. However, Joanna put up a fuss. Not that it got her anywhere.

Tom and Joanna got married and, six months later, Joanna had her first baby--a baby girl they named Ruthann. Things were bad from the beginning since Tom was forced to marry Joanna. He would tell Joanna that his life was ruined because she went and got "knocked up." She should have been smart and used something. Joanna, who was a strong willed girl, would tell you exactly what she was thinking, and she made no bones about it. Tom and Joanna argued all the time but Joanna really wanted the marriage to work, and she worked hard at her marriage. She would always make sure Tom had something to eat, his clothes were clean, and they had a clean house. She kept herself up and she kept Ruthann looking good. Joanna didn't want her marriage to fail; she loved Tom and she wanted Tom to be happy. Eventually, Joanna began to lose herself little by little. She put all of her dreams on the back burner and she attended to Tom with every fiber of her being. During their marriage, Joanna gave birth to three more girls. She was taking care of Tom, the kids and the house. Tom began to work late hours at work. Joanna found herself alone quite a bit. She thought, *If I change, maybe that will work; if I do*

more for him and give him more of myself maybe that might work;
if I be a better wife maybe that might work as well." Oh, she put
a mask on her face and hid everything very well. She would
tell Mama that everything was fine, but Mama knew better.
Mama would always tell Joanna, "Baby, I am here if you ever
want to talk." Joanna would put that smile on her face and
say, "No, Mama, everything is fine."

Joanna was carrying such a big burden within her, it was
tearing her up inside. She attended to Tom and the kids' every
need. She had little time for herself. She pushed herself and
pushed herself to make a good marriage. The only problem
was that Joanna was pushing by herself. Joanna began to notice a difference in Tom's behavior. He started to work later
and later. On one occasion, Joanna wanted to surprise Tom.
She cooked an extremely elegant meal for the two of them and
made his favorite dessert. The table was set with candles all
around. However, Tom came home late and Joanna waited up
for him. When Tom entered the house, Joanna noticed he had
one of the biggest smiles on his face. When Tom saw Joanna,
his face quickly turned sour.

"What are you doing up?" he asked. "Waiting for you, we
need to talk-I need to know what's going on."

He quickly replied, "Joanna, I am tired, I'm going to bed."

"Tom, I prepared your favorite dinner and made your favorite dessert. I have been cooking for hours. I wanted us to
have a special evening together, to spend some time together
without the kids. Tom, I did this for you, I worked for hours in
the kitchen trying to cook you something special. Look, look
at what I did, I did all this for you, for you Tom."

Tom looked around and saw the table beautifully set with

his favorite dinner and dessert. The candles had burned out. Tom replied, "I'm tired, I'm going to bed."

As he was walking to the bedroom, Joanna called out, "Tom?" He turned around. "When you walked into the house, you had a big smile on your face—what was that all about?"

"Uh, nothing, nothing, I was just glad to get home," he replied.

Joanna sat on the couch; she knew something wasn't right. Yet, within herself, she really didn't want or was not ready for the truth. Joanna's burden began to get bigger and bigger. Tom continued to come home late. He began to want more time to himself. He distanced himself from Joanna. He was a busy man without Joanna. Finally, Joanna decided to go and talk to Mama. She opened up and told Mama everything that was going on. To her surprise, Mama didn't judge her and she wasn't surprised by what Joanna had said. Momma was right there for Joanna with love and words of wisdom. She said, "Joanna, I know that your heart has been troubled. I have been praying for you that God would give you wisdom. If you believe within your heart that something isn't right, you need to talk to your man. I mean, make him give you some answers and don't you take what he says lightly and just say, 'okay'. You pray before you have that talk with your man and ask God to let the truth be revealed--to prepare your heart for what you believe you know so that you are ready for the answers. If you really want to know, the God of Truth will reveal some things to you, but, Joanna you gotta be ready to hear." Joanna listened to Mama. Joanna began to rethink some things in her mind, the little things that she let go by because she was afraid of the truth. Joanna prayed and prayed.

One evening, when Tom came home, Joanna was ready within her heart and she had overcome all of her fears. She believed that Tom was messing around on her. As a matter of fact, she knew he was. But Joanna had to get to the place that she was ready to hear; that was going to be the hard part. She had put her man first above everyone and everything. She built herself around his world. She danced to his music. She fought the hardest to get the marriage going. She endured hard negative words from Tom who would later apologize for the things he said to her. She lost more and more of herself. Why? Because she did not want to be alone, she wanted her marriage to work. She loved Tom and she loved him hard. She gave her all and all, but he didn't. But now she was ready; she was ready to hear the truth. She had listened to Momma, who told her what the Bible says about marriage. She had given her all. Joanna told Tom they needed to talk.

After a while they began to talk, not argue. They were not on the defensive; they just talked. Because Joanna had prayed and asked God to reveal the truth, her petition was honored. Tom was open with Joanna and told her all the truth. He had been seeing a woman, he loved this woman, he rented her an apartment, and he wanted to be with her. Joanna listened intently. After Tom had told it all, Joanna had the strength to tell Tom that she loved him, but she knew something was wrong and she had worked hard in trying to make her marriage work for their family. Joanna told Tom to go to other woman. "You can't have her and have me too," she said. "I care too much for myself to succumb to a low level; I have pride and dignity. I cannot allow myself to be used no longer. I can make it and I WILL make it. I know it's going to be hard but I am gonna make it. I know that I've done the right thing and I tried to make this marriage work for you, the kids and me. I might shed some tears, I might have some sleepless nights, and maybe some restless days, but I am gonna make it. At times, I may be lonely and just go through the motions, but I am gonna make it."

Tom was shocked because Joanna wasn't stressed out; she spoke calmly with an authoritative voice. She continued on, "I have given you my all and all. You see, Tom, a person will only do what you allow them to do and I allowed you to walk all over me. I kept making excuses because of my own fears. I let you get away with things and I knew better. I was dedicated to you, I loved you. I wanted you, and I wanted to be with you. I thought we made it through the bad times, but I see I was only lying to myself.

"Tom, you messed up and you messed up bad. You couldn't be a man and come and talk to me. No, you had to sneak around. I tried and God knows I tried. You decided not to keep your vows you made to me; you promised to love me and be faithful to me. But you lied, Tom, you lied. You cheated yourself out of a good thing. You lost the best thing that ever happened to you. One day, you're going to look back and you're going to remember this conversation. You're going to remember what a cheater and liar you were, and you're going to remember that I was the best thing that ever happened to you. So, you can leave my house now, right now. No need to get your stuff, just get out."

Tom left the house, but he couldn't figure out for the life of him why he told Joanna the truth. What he didn't know was that Joanna had prayed and asked God that the truth be revealed. God granted her petition. He also didn't know that Joanna had spoken with Mama, who told her to use wisdom and to be led by the Holy Spirit.

As Tom left, Joanna fell on the couch and cried her heart out. She sobbed loudly and she cried, and cried and cried. Her pain was so deep that words cannot describe it. Her heart felt like it was hurting and it did hurt. She had given so much of herself to her marriage and she allowed things to go on because she did not have the courage or strength to say "Stop it!" She allowed her man to walk all over her.

As time went on, Joanna had good days and bad days. She had her ups and her downs. Joanna didn't like being alone and she felt that she needed a man. Every now and then, she would think about Tom. He was able to see the kids every other weekend and some holidays. Tom had moved on and gotten married again. Joanna allowed both some bitterness and some self-esteem into her heart. Eventually, she found another man and married her second husband. Joanna still wanted to love and be loved, so she married a man who she thought she loved. This was Mr. Right. He did everything for Joanna and she wanted for nothing. Whatever she needed or thought she needed or wanted, he provided for her. He gave her everything except for time. Her second husband was a successful businessman, his name was John. John was all business; he had a pleasant personality and attitude. John loved to feel the energy, he loved excitement, and he was adventurous. John had a secret—his job was his first wife. Very soon, Joanna found herself all alone. Even though John was there, he was successful in his business but he had little time for Joanna. He would promise Joanna that he would spend more time with her. But every time something else came up: he had to meet clients, he had to call clients, and he had to email his clients and had to send this proposal or that proposal. It was always his job. This led to Joanna's second divorce. The burden deepened, the bitterness grew even more, and the low self-esteem increased. Joanna began to drink to ease her pain.

One evening, Joanna's friends asked her to come along to 'Happy Hour." At first, Joanna declined but eventually gave in and joined her friends. Joanna was not the happy girl that she once was. She was bitter and she began to drink more and more to ease her pain. Joanna found herself in a self-pity mood, and soon was traveling on a self-destructive road.

This time, Joanna met a slick, fast talking guy. He talked and talked and talked Joanna into marrying him. He became what Joanna wanted, not what she needed. He gave her all the time in the world. But his lifestyle was fast; and Joanna was not as fast as Rick, her third husband. Joanna was wild with Rick and she felt free with him. She did not have to pretend or work hard at their marriage; Rick was what Joanna wanted. Rick stayed in the clubs and everybody knew Rick. He was cool. He walked the walk and talked the talk. He would go into the club and everybody would greet him and Joanna loudly. This was the fast lifestyle and Joanna loved it. During the day, Rick and Joanna did nothing, but when nighttime fell they came alive. Joanna had a large divorce settlement from her first husband, Tom, and an even larger divorce settlement from John. She had plenty of money and Rick knew it. Oh, Rick was there at Joanna's call. He gave her all the time she wanted. He made her feel good about herself, he loved her with passion, and he put her first. For the first time, she felt as though she deserved it. But, Rick was slick. He knew exactly what he was doing. Mama tried to warn her; and her sister, Susan, tried to warn her, but Joanna wouldn't listen.

Joanna dressed Rick in the finest clothes and she dressed in the finest clothes. They partied like there was no tomorrow. Rick treated Joanna like a queen. He always told her how fine she was, how smart she was, how she rocked his world, and he could not live without her. He built her ego up; she no longer had low self-esteem about herself. Rick made her feel good; he made her feel good all over. When they walked in the club, everybody knew her; everybody knew that she was Rick's woman. She was in the spotlight and she loved all the attention. When Rick had Joanna right where he wanted her, and he felt the time was right, he slyly introduced her to cocaine. She declined at first, but he told her how good it would make her feel. She trusted Rick and she felt good with Rick. Yes, she gave in to him. He showed her what to do, he egged her on, he talked the talk and she fell right into the trap.

He then began to teach her about the other street drugs and the ups and how tos. He continued to be at her call, he continued to tell her how fine she was, how smart she was, that she rocked his world and he couldn't live without her. He slyly began to increase the amount of drugs she was using and slowly he began to control. Mama tried to talk to her and make her see, to even get her help. Her sister, Susan, tried to help her. She wouldn't let anyone in, no one except for Rick. She said Rick made her feel like a woman, he made her feel good about herself. Her family tried to tell her that Rick was only using her. She would get upset and leave, always saying, "You don't know Rick. You don't know how he makes me feel. He treats me like I am somebody; he spends time with me, he sees about me and I am the one that rocks his world."

Mama would tell her, "He don't care about you, he just wants to spend all your money and get you more hooked up on drugs." When Joanna left Mama's house, she said to herself, "They don't understand. Rick is my man and he makes me feel good all over."

One day, Joanna couldn't find Rick. He had always been there, she always knew where he was, he always let her know where he was going. *Where is he now? How come I can't find him? Where's Rick?* All those insecure thoughts quickly flooded her mind. She went to their club, their spot, where she was always in the spotlight, and she walked into the room. People called her name, "Joanna, Ms. Fine Joanna." But, this time as she walked through the club, thoughts of low self-esteem overwhelmed her.

For the first time in years, she felt lost. She knew something was wrong. For the first time, she couldn't find Rick, for the first time he was out of pocket. He was not there to answer her every call, to see if she needed anything or to ask what she wanted. Joanna was furious. She walked into the club, but this time everyone looked at her as though they knew something, but what? She felt overwhelmed with thoughts of low self-esteem; all eyes were on her. Someone shouted out, "Joanna, Ms. Fine Joanna!"

She looked around the club, and lo and behold, she spotted Rick. But, what, who-who is he sitting with?

"Rick, where were you? Where have you been?" Rick was sitting at the table with Lil Man. "Oh, I was helping Lil Man out today; he needed some help with something. You were sleeping and I didn't want to wake you up."

Joanna said, "I've been calling you all day and you haven't returned any of my calls, not one." Lil Man left the table. Rick slyly said to Joanna, "I don't have to tell you where I am going."

She looked at Rick with amazement. "What did you say?" she asked.

"Ah, come on, baby, you know I was just with Lil Man; I told you I was helping him out. Come on girl, you know you are fine, smart and you are the only one that rocks my world. You know that, don't you? Nobody, but you baby, nobody but you. Girl, you are mine with your fine self." Joanna fell for it; she fell right into the trap. He handed her something small in a pouch and told her, "This will make you feel good." Joanna just had to ask Rick the million dollar question, "You love me, don't you?"

He responded, "Yeah baby, you know I do." As the night went on, Joanna was happy in the arms of her man. Little did she know that she was in deep over her head.

Rick began to give Joanna more and more drugs; and he began to take away the one thing that Joanna thought she wanted, which was time with her man. Time was very important to Joanna, because in her first marriage, she had given her all, and that time was taken away from her by another woman. In her second marriage, she had a successful man with a successful job, but he spent the majority of his time on that job trying to keep and multiply what he already had. That time was taken away from her by her husband's job. Now, when she met Rick, he gave her all the time she thought she wanted. The enemy had set a trap. Joanna noticed how Rick was pulling away from her more and more, how he now had the control over her. She was now dependent upon Rick for drugs and the little time she was getting. Her burden was now bigger, deeper, wider and the weight of it was getting heavier and heavier. Mama insisted that she go into rehab, but Joanna refused. Rick stopped telling Joanna that she was fine, smart and she was the only one who rocked his world. Those words were long gone. He started telling her she was a mess.

He would say, "You used to be fine and smart. But just look at you now, nothing but a mess." The words cut through Joanna like a piercing sword. She was devastated. She was now hooked on drugs and that was all she thought about day in and day out. Her money had dwindled down to nothing. She had pushed her family away. She was alone. The enemy had set a trap. Needless to say, once all the money was gone, so was Rick.

She felt worthless and hopeless. She took more drugs to ease her pain, but the pain would not go away. Joanna was now homeless. The burden she was carrying she was now dragging. She had no strength left and she felt useless. But Joanna kept going. She kept looking and searching. She kept taking more and more drugs. She wanted the drugs to take all of her pain away. But that made it worse. Meanwhile, Mama was a praying woman. She kept her daughter lifted up in the Lord. She asked the Lord to protect her and let no hurt or harm come to her. She asked God to send His laborers across Joanna's path, so seeds could be planted in her heart. She even asked God to bring Joanna to the end of herself, so she could call on the name of Jesus for herself. Mama would say, "Lord, bring her to the end of herself, before the enemy tries to take her out. Lord, bring her to the end of herself, so when she calls you, she can find you for herself. Lord, she needs to know you for herself. Father, in the midst of it all, I know that you are able to deliver my child out of the hand of the enemy." Mama kept that prayer before the Lord; she never gave up praying for her daughter. Mama believed in the power of prayer, she believed in God's Word. She knew that God would work on behalf of His Word, and His Word would not come back void. He would watch over his Word.

Time went on and Joanna got worse. One Friday night, Joanna ended up in jail and she spent the whole weekend in jail. When they released her on Monday, Joanna went straight to the crack house. There, she found someone who gave her what she needed, although it would cost her. Eventually, Joanna moved in with a drug dealer and she began to steal his drugs. When the dealer found out, he beat Joanna so bad that she ended up in the hospital with broken bones. Mama found out what happened and went to the hospital to see about her daughter. Once she entered the room, the first thing she did was rebuke the devil from her daughter. She spoke the words of life into her daughter. She prayed scriptures over her daughter, she spoke God's promises over her daughter, and she loved on her daughter. Joanna was still not ready to see the light. When Joanna got out of the hospital, again, she went straight to the crack house.

One day, when Joanna was getting high, she remembered the words Mama prayed over her, "I declare in the name of Jesus you are healed from the top of your head to the soles of your feet. No more, no more will the enemy have control over you. Your eyes will be opened so you can see and your ears will be unplugged so you can hear the Gospel of Jesus Christ."

Joanna thought, "Wow." Then, she heard a voice say, "You are fearfully and wonderfully made. You are Mine and no one can snatch you out of My hand." Joanna rubbed her eyes and thought she was hallucinating.

That same day, Joanna was on her way back to the crack house. A young lady stopped Joanna on the street and said, "May I speak with you for a moment?"

Joanna said, "Yeah, if you got some money."

The young lady responded, "Yes, I do. I have all the money I need and more than enough. My daddy owns it all." The young lady hurriedly spoke before Joanna would walk away. She said, "As you walked by, the Lord told me to tell you that you are fearfully and wonderfully made, you are His and no one can snatch you out of His hand."

Joanna's eyes filled with tears. The young lady continued on and said, "I don't know what you're going through, but God knows and He has a plan and purpose for your life. When you get tired of doing what you are doing, all you have to do is call on the name of Jesus for yourself." Joanna looked at the girl and said, "Mama told me the same thing, just call on Him, call His name." But Joanna turned away from the young lady and said, "Yeah, yeah, yeah, right," and walked off quickly.

Joanna continued to do her thing. She was out there and she was out there bad. She was going from dope house to dope house and everyone knew Joanna. Joanna was tired and her body was telling her that it had suffered enough. Joanna wouldn't listen to her body; she kept going on and on. Several days later, Joanna put the pipe to her lips in a strange room with a strange man. She heard a voice say, "You are fearfully and wonderfully made, you are Mine and no one can snatch you out of My hand." Joanna broke down and cried and cried and cried. She was so tired and downtrodden. The burden she carried now carried her. She looked around at the mess she was in and she wondered how she got there. Again, Joanna heard a voice say, "You are Mine and no one snatch you out of My hand, because you are fearfully and wonderfully made." Again, Joanna broke down. With her lips trembling and her body shaking, Joanna heard herself say, "Jesus, I heard about you but I don't know you for myself. Mama said all I have to do is call on the name of Jesus saying, 'Jesus help me'." At that moment, her body went into a slump. She was unconscious. The strange man who was in the room looked at Joanna and saw she was unresponsive and he thought she had overdosed. He called 911 and quickly left the room. Joanna was taken to hospital with a very weak pulse and shallow breathing. In the emergency room, they worked on Joanna and she began to slowly respond.

Meanwhile, Mama had heard what happened. She called one of her closest friends and said, "Pray for Joanna." That's all she had to say to her friend, and her friend didn't ask any questions. She prayed for Joanna as if she were her own daughter. Mama called on God's promises and reminded God of His promise to her. She opened her mouth wide and she let the words come out. "Lord, your Word says..." and she went on and on. She did not fall with terror, but she believed on God's promises and she put her trust in the Lord. Joanna was released from the emergency room floor and sent up to the Intensive Care Unit. It did not look good. Joanna's body had been through so much. Joanna was in a coma for some days. Around her bedside, the family stayed and they filled her room with prayer, hymns, and praises unto the Lord. The nurses couldn't believe that the family was singing at a time like this. Didn't they know that this was serious? Didn't they know that Joanna was hanging on by a thread? Didn't they know? Mama knew. She knew that when the praises go up, the blessings come down. She knew about the power of prayer. As she prayed over her daughter and anointed her daughter with oil, she again gave God's promises back to Him and she thanked God for saving her daughter. Several days went by, and Joanna came out of the coma. She didn't know all that had happened, she didn't know all the prayers that went up to God for her, she didn't know that she almost didn't make it. But when she came to, in a soft voice she whispered, "Jesus." The room filled with praises, filled with "Thank you, Jesus" and the room was full of songs. It took Joanna a good while before she got out of the hospital because her body had been so beaten down, so broken down with the drugs and the life that she led. Joanna did not look her age, she looked older; the hard life she led and the drugs had deteriorated her body.

Joanna left the hospital and was transferred to the Rehab Ward. There, she got better; it was a difficult and continued to be a difficult journey for her. But she learned for herself to call on the name of Jesus. She learned, for herself, the power in the name of Jesus. She now knew who Jesus was for herself. With all that she had been through, she thanked God for watching over her and keeping her from all hurt and harm. She learned for herself that she could have a relationship with Jesus. She became a strong Christian, who got filled with the power of the Holy Spirit. She began telling her story of how the enemy set a trap for her and how she fell into the trap. How she had to carry her burden and the burden became so heavy that, eventually, the burden was carrying her; pushing her along. The ride got faster and faster and she didn't know how to get off. She told her story, and she let women know that you don't need a man to make you feel whole. You don't need to become dependent upon a man, drugs, anyone or anything else to make you feel better about yourself. She also spoke of time, and stated that what she wanted was time with her man. She thought that was what she needed, but it was just a want; a want to fulfill the void that was in her life.

She went on to say, "I found a man, a real man, who provides for me and fulfills all of my needs. I no longer have to look in the streets or the crack house. I no longer have to feel worthless or hopeless. I don't need all the attention. I don't need all the material stuff. I don't need the drugs or the pain of it all. I don't need bitterness and hatred. I don't need your sympathy about the life I led or your sympathy about the things that I went through. I don't need your judgmental eyes staring down at me. I don't need the hypocrisy. I don't need the stares or the giggles about what I have been through. I don't need your pious pity. What I need is Jesus and I called on the name of Jesus for myself. Jesus is the name above all names. Beautiful, Savior, Glorious Lord. Jesus is the lover of my soul. Jesus, I will never let you go. You've taken me from the miry clay and you've set my feet upon the rock that I now know. I love you, I need you, though my world may fall, I'll never let you go, My Savior, my closest friend, I will worship you until the very end. As Mama said, 'I am healed from the top of my head to the soles of my feet'. I am free!"

As Susan drove, she realized how much she loved her sister and said with a glad heart, "Well, that sister of mine has come a long way. Now she's whole and set free, and now she wants to control me. She has been through a lot and now she wants to try and control me. Lord, I am almost to the hospital. I have about forty-five minutes to go. Lord, please spare Mama. Let me be able to see Mama."

As Susan turned into the hospital, her heart was racing. As she got closer and closer, she could see a hearse and they were loading a body into it. She hurriedly parked the car and told her kids to come on as she was running to the hospital entrance. Tears streamed down her face. She heard herself saying, "Lord, I asked you to let me see Mama. Why is this happening?" She looked behind her to see if her kids were keeping up. They didn't understand what's going on and why she was running so hard and fast.

Finally, Susan made it inside the hospital. Her heart was racing, dancing and pumping fast. She was out of breath. Her stomach was turning inside and out. She found the elevator and made it to the floor. Her eyes were darting left and right, up and down the hall to find the room. She didn't know what to expect or what to do. She finally found the room. She looked into the room and saw Mama lying in the bed. She heard herself saying, "Thank you, Jesus." She broke down and cried, hurrying to Mama's side. Joanna entered the room and said, "Susan, Mama is going to be alright. We fell into each other arms and cried and loved on our mama.

Joanna was a changed woman because she had an encounter with Jesus that changed her life forever. The enemy came and tried to steal, kill and destroy Joanna. She did things and allowed things to be done to her. She allowed herself to be used by men, have low self-esteem about herself, and carry a burden for years and years that she was not supposed to carry. She became a slave to the thing that she feared the most, being alone. When Joanna's first husband left her for another woman, she felt worthless and hopeless. She vowed that it would never happen to her again. She had given so much of herself and in the process, she lost who she was. Insecurities crept in, low self-esteem was upon her and she didn't feel as pretty as she used to. Oh, she put up a good front; no one ever knew the emptiness and pain that she felt. She would go to work and be around her friends, laughing and smiling on the outside but dying on the inside. She didn't know Jesus, so she didn't know how to give that burden to Him. She carried it around and the burden got bigger and bigger. Eventually, the burden was drowning Joanna. She had been hurt, and hurt badly. She did not allow herself to fully grieve for the failing of her marriages. No, she was too strong for that, and she wanted everyone to know just how strong she was. But behind closed doors, that's when the tears would overtake her, that's when the emptiness set in, that's when the sleepless nights rolled in. However, through it all, when she called on the name of Jesus, that's when He delivered her and made possible a life of peace and wholeness. Jesus was the one who had given Joanna so much. She was able to live again and to love again.

You see, anyone can have a burden; but we are not to carry our burdens. We are to give our burdens to the Lord. Mama had a burden for her child, seeing her child go through what she was going through was not easy for her.

Your burden could be sickness in your body, going through

a tough trial, being tested, being confused, tired of going through bad times. If you have ever been lonely or felt hopeless, worthless, yet pasted a smile on your face when you felt torn on the inside, then this is for you. Have you ever felt like you didn't know what to do, but felt that something needed to be done? This is for women who feel they don't belong and want to belong. For the women who have sons or daughters on drugs, lost family members, the broken down, the depressed, the women who have sickness in their bodies, divorced women, single moms, women who are fighting for their marriages. This is for women who think that Jesus couldn't love them, women just trying to make ends meet, for women who have bitterness, who have insecurities, who feel that they are stagnant in their spiritual walk, for women who need a touch from the Lord. This is for women who have a song in their hearts, but don't know how to sing it; for women who have a dance in their feet, but their feet won't move.

God's Word says, "Fear not, for I have redeemed you; I have called you by your name; you are Mine. When you pass through the waters, I will be with you; and through the rivers, they shall not overflow you. When you walk through the fire, you shall not be burned, nor shall the flame scorch you. For I am the Lord, your God" (Isaiah 43:1-3).

Always remember that Jesus loves you! Psalm 139:14 says, "I will praise You, for I am fearfully and wonderfully made. Marvelous are Your works. How precious also are Your thoughts to me." John 10:28 says, "Jesus always has you on His mind and nobody can snatch you out of His hand."

Hold on ladies, this is the year. Hold on.

F.E.A.R.

Woot is Fear? How does Fear get a hold on you? Fear comes in many disguises; fear can grip you and fill you with anxiety and stress. When Fear grips you, if not dealt with, it can cause sickness. Fear can cause you to have panic attacks. Fear can make you lose your focus, and fear can keep you captive and make you a prisoner. What does God say about fear? "For God has not given us a spirit of fear, but of power, love and a sound mind" (2ⁿᵈ Timothy 1:7).

"I sought the Lord and He heard me, and delivered me from all my fears" (Psalm 34:4).

"And He said, 'O man, greatly beloved, fear not! Peace be to you, be strong, yes be strong!'" (Daniel 10:19)

At one time or another, we all have faced fear. If we are honest with ourselves, we could have had fear of being alone, fear of failing, fear of new challenges, fear of not getting a promotion, losing a job, fear of marriage, divorce, raising kids--the list could go on and on. But, again, I say, if we are honest with ourselves, at one time or another, we all have faced fear.

We have to proclaim God's words over our fears. When fear comes knocking at your door, you open the door whole-heartedly. You want to invite fear in. I believe it's easier to invite fear in, than to look at fear and say, "Back off!" When you let fear in, you are ready and willing to say to yourself, "I'm afraid." Why? That's what the enemy wants us to do. Satan wants us to be so fearful and afraid, that we won't proclaim God's promises, God's Word. It's easier to hide our fears than to look our fears in the face and say, "With the help of God, I can deal with this. I can overcome this." In order for us to do that, we have to take a deep look at ourselves and get to the root, the real reason why we are afraid: why we choose to walk in fear. At times, this is not easy. We will have to be ready to look at ourselves and see the flaw in our character that God will show us. This is good when we choose to look at our fears in the face and ask God to deliver us from the fear. That is a major step. As I continue to look at fear, the scripture clearly states that, "Fear involves torment" (1 John 4:18). Why is this? It is because, at that point, we let fear, "The Fear" control us so that it can torment us. It will continually rear its head up, never letting us rest in that area. Fear will tell you, "You can't do that, it's out of your league." Then you don't even try and you have the fear of failure. The Holy Spirit speaks to you and tells you to give someone words of encouragement. Fear speaks to you and says you don't even know that person. An opportunity comes your way for you to own your own business; fear tells you that you don't have the knowledge or skills to start that business. A seed of doubt is planted and you talk yourself out of the idea. You avoid the idea that God just gave you. You pray over your children, fear tells you to give up. The

Holy Spirit tells you to forgive someone; fear says they won't accept your apology. You continuously let fear guide you. Fear is from the enemy, to keep you fearful and afraid to pursue the things of God, afraid to be whole. Fear is a lie from the enemy.

Fear is:

Ferocious
Enemy
Attack Against
Righteous

Ferocious Enemy Attack Against the Righteous. That's what fear is. We as Christians have no place in our lives for fear. We have God's Word. "But, now, thus says the LORD, who created you, 'O' Jacob, and He who formed you, O Israel, fear not, for I have redeemed you" (Isaiah 43:1).

In our lives as Christians we are free; we are delivered and we have the victory. When fear comes our way and knocks on the door, do not invite fear in; proclaim God's promises over your life and speak God's Word. Put your faith into action. We have to truly depend on God. Give this fear over to God. Don't let fear linger on you or in you. Put fear out and shut the door on fear. Tell fear it has no place in your life because you are redeemed; you are righteous in Christ Jesus.

We give fear so much room to grow that it overpowers us and we let fear have control. We let fear torment us to the point of being afraid. So we don't do anything but hold fear up. Once we truly and sincerely look at our fears, give our fear to the Lord, and trust in the Lord, then we overcome that fear.

We then go out and do what God has been calling us to do or say. That fear held us captive but it no longer has any power over our lives. Praise God for His strength and for His power. Praise God. Don't let fear rule you. God will strengthen the weak hand and make firm the feeble knees.

Trusting in the Lord

As we go through our trials and tribulations, we should always learn from what we are going through. We can also learn by watching others who are going through their tests. Watching one particular woman, I've learned some important lessons from her.

This lady is beautiful inside and out. When she walks, her walk is with dignity. When she speaks, her words are full of love. When she smiles, it is like a ray of sunshine, so beautiful and bright. When she laughs, her laughter touches your inner soul. When she looks at you, her beautiful brown eyes seem as though they can see right through you. When she touches you, you feel safe and secure. When she dresses herself in her richly fine clothes, you do not find vanity or deceit in her wardrobe. And, when she gives, she gives with all of her heart and never withholds anything. Her life is so full and rich. She lives each day to its fullest. She relies and depends on her Lord, her Savior, Jesus Christ. She is a strong black woman who is not afraid to shed her tears. She is so confident, she is not afraid to share her deepest feelings with you. Fear is not in her vocabulary. She will never hurt you or tear you down with words; her gentle spirit is to uplift you and encourage you. Her love will overpower you; her joy will overtake you, and her peace she quietly gives to you. You will find goodness in her day to day living. When she smiles, you can see her kindness. She never loses her patience. She is faithful to her family and friends. Her gentleness will put you at ease, so that you feel as though you can share anything with her. Longsuffering, she endures. She hopes and trusts in her loving Savior. She knows her strength came from Him. This beautiful woman trusts in the Lord with all her heart, all her soul, and all her mind.

This woman and her life reflect that she is a child of God. When she was in her younger years, she decided to change careers. She quit her job and decided to become a nurse. She had a husband and two young daughters. She began to go to school for nursing. Her homework was taking a lot of time from her family, yet she learned to balance family, school, and have time for her husband. She had to learn so much and pass every class. I've never seen determination as I have seen in this lady. Her every hour she was in her books, or at school, and trying to balance it all. She had to help her daughters with their homework, continue to teach them, and see to her husband. Determination was a part of her as never before. This woman of God walked across that stage on graduation day and her family was there to see her get her nursing degree and her nursing pin. She was pinned to become a nurse and she wore her pin proudly. She was walking in what God had called her to do. With a loving heart, a gentle sprit, meekness, and in kindness, she gave her all to her patients.

One of the ways God blessed this family was financially. This family moved from one part of town to the other. Her daughters attended parochial school and they began to take piano lessons. This woman and her husband bought one of the finest pianos ever for their daughters. They began to go downtown for music lessons at the best music school. This lady was walking in God's favor and she was passing the blessing on to others. In this woman's house, I have seen family members and friends come from near and far for this couple to help them. They fed anyone and everyone who came to their house, and if they could help financially, they would. I've seen family members and friends stop by for encouraging words, to tell this woman their secrets, which they felt they could only share with her. Seeing her gentleness and her faithfulness, they were able to confide in this woman of God. She shared her time, not holding back.

Oh, don't think that the lady's life was so easy. She had a lot to endure. When she was approximately thirteen years of age, she was told that she had Rubella Fever, which is a heart condition. She never let her heart condition stop her. As a matter of fact, you would never know she had a heart condition. Years later, after her firstborn son, her doctor told her that she should not have any more kids. Not listening to the doctor, many years later, she got pregnant and suffered a miscarriage. Determined, years later, this woman of God was to try again and the doctors told her that she might not make it, due to her heart condition. Her heart was "too weak to go through labor," so they said. But this woman of God had a second child, and despite what the doctors said, she bore a beautiful baby girl.

This woman of God made it and her baby made it. She believed in the Creator who created the heavens and the earth. She believed in Jesus Christ to strengthen her. Her baby was born on November 10th, and she named her baby girl, Pamela Marie. "With men this is impossible, but with God all things are possible" (Matthew 19:26). Two years later, she bore her third child, another beautiful baby girl, whom she named Vanessa Theresa. She overcame the obstacles, she overcame what the doctor had said she should and could not do. When her oldest daughter was in the 5th grade, this lady (whom I will now refer to as Barbara, my mama) went into the hospital for her heart. This was her test, her trial. Barbara overcame that and came home to her family. She endured and began to continue her life to the fullest, not letting her heart condition stop her or letting the fear rule her.

Barbara pursued her careers and her education. She went from working at a radio station, to reception operator, to social worker for the welfare division, to going to school for nursing and graduating, receiving her pin for nursing. She went from working in a hospital, to private duty, to a clinic, back to private duty. She loved what she was doing, and it showed in her life, all while tending to her home, her husband, her children and raising her grandson. She did all of this while working on her nursing career and giving time to her family and friends.

One day, this woman of God suffered a stroke. She was immediately rushed to the hospital. Her family was devastated. She stayed in the hospital for a while. Determination had set in again. Barbara was determined to get over this. With the help of God, she overcame, and was back to her normal routine. She never let her heart guide her steps. She lived her life to the fullest. Barbara traveled with her sisters on many, many occasions. She continued to dress. Never did she let conceit or vanity come anywhere near her. Over the years, Barbara continued to go to church, and was in her missionary group at the church. Barbara was doing fine. She was working for the Lord, going to church and continuing on with her nursing career. In June of '74, Barbara was told that she would have to have open heart surgery; her heart was getting weaker. That month, her daughter, Pam, was about to graduate from St. Mel High School. Again, this family was devastated. Barbara's husband, (my daddy), was in a wheelchair, recovering and my mama was in the hospital. On the day of my graduation, neither my Mother nor my Father was able to attend. But, I had an aunt who was always there with me and for me in my time of distress and need. Determination set in again. God was using my mother through her illness to show the family that you must have faith in the Lord. No matter what it looks like, you have to trust in the Lord. She never complained. She kept on moving. She kept on living. She kept on trusting in the Lord. She was determined to live, not let her heart rule her or let fear grip her. Barbara was released from the hospital; she was able to continue to do the things she loved. She relied on the Lord to strengthen her; God used her in many ways. The doctors did not know how she kept going. "Not by might, nor by power, but the Spirit of God" (Zechariah 4:6). Time went on and years passed. Barbara saw her daughters grow into beautiful young ladies. She saw her grandkids. She continued to live for the Lord. She continued to encourage and uplift her family and friends. She continued to show them that if you want it bad enough, you have to go after it. You cannot let your trials hold you down; just trust and believe in the Lord.

Over the years, Barbara (my mama) had another stroke. She made it through, she came out. Again, determination set in. Now, it appeared that Barbara's heart was getting weaker and weaker. Her doctors told her that she would need to be opened up again, for valves to be placed in her heart. Devastation struck our family yet again. My mom went into the hospital to have the valves put in. My daddy was scared; sister, brother and I were scared. Fear had gripped us. While we were scared, I know my mama was praying. She was asking God to strengthen her one more time. My Mama had the valves put in and was released from the hospital. Determination had set in. Did she slow down? No. She continued to live life to the fullest, but now she was slowing down on her job. Eventually, she stopped working. She did not let her heart stop her, or rule her, or guide her. She lived life and lived for the Lord. She blessed her family in more ways than one can imagine. Sometime later, my mama had another stroke. This time, the stroke affected her speech. She came out of the stroke but had to go to speech therapy. She worked hard in therapy to get her speech back. She did not stop there; she continued on. She was determined to live her life. She loved life and she lived it to the fullest.

I wrote this story in loving memory of my mom. She was my best friend, my inspiration. She loved the Lord and she loved life. Others would have complained and complained and made life miserable for those around them. But my mom was special. She did not let her illness stop her in any way. She moved on, she lived and lived life to the fullest. She taught her daughters how to live their lives for the Lord; she taught us how to pray. When things got hard, she would direct us to the Lord. On one occasion, when I was going through one of my hard times, my mom gave me a little white Bible, and she wrote in it, "Pam, Faith, hope and Trust. Barbara, your Mother." As I write this, my heart is overwhelmed. The tears, my tears are flowing down my face. I can still feel her love, her peace. I see her so clearly. Oh, I thank God that He gave me my mama: a mother to nourish me, to instill priceless values in me. She was letting me know to always have faith, hope and to trust the Lord, no matter what. What a gift, what a joy, what a blessing.

That's my story of my beloved mother, whom I love and cherish. My mama was a praying mother. With everything she went through, she prayed, and God was faithful to her. He was the one that instilled in her to live life to the fullest. To love life.

TESTIMONY: For a period of time, I was out of the church. My mama and sister prayed for me during this time. My father was out of the church and my mother prayed for daddy to come back to the Lord. My mama is gone on with the Lord now, but because of her prayers, my father and I are both where we belong. If you are praying for a lost one and you do not see a glimmer of hope, you keep on praying. No matter what, you pray on for that lost soul. God hears and answers prayers. Pray on, because God is faithful. Amen.

A Mother's Story, God's hand of Mercy

I awoke to a beautiful day; the sun was bursting with its beauty and playing peek-a-boo, dancing through my bedroom window. As I prepared myself for the day's activities, I thanked God for this day, slid out of bed, and took care of my personal grooming. I got my first cup of hot coffee, and walked out of my front door to soak in all of God's beauty. As I sipped my coffee I heard the birds singing. It was a beautiful day, the sun shone brightly, the trees looked as though they were taking their morning stretch, the limbs with all the green leaves looked exceptionally beautiful this morning. The lawns were manicured just right. I continued to sip my coffee as the neighbors passed by, some jogging and some walking their dogs. Oh, what a beautiful day!

This day was Saturday, May 15, 1999. My son, Joseph Marcus, would be preparing himself for his senior prom. Parked in front of our house was a white sports utility van that Joseph Marcus wanted for his prom. As I looked at this vehicle I noticed the size of it, and thought to myself *It's pretty big.* The thought left my mind, and I came back into the house. This was going to be a beautiful Saturday--so much to do. An hour or so later my daughter, grandson and I left the house for our regular Saturday adventures. As we were driving and just taking in the beautiful the day, we laughed, talked, and occasionally my grandson broke in with a gurgle.

As time went on, we had to cancel some appointments; this day was flying by. I promised my son I would be home by 5:00 that evening. Well, we made the deadline, and were home by 5:00. The phone was ringing off the hook. Entering into the house was Joseph Marcus with his tux in his hands. While waiting on Joseph Marcus to dress, the phone rang and it was my cousin from Chicago calling to say hi. Out of the corner of my eye, I caught a glimpse of Joseph Marcus standing in the doorway. I looked my son up and down; the boy was "sharp." I then described to my cousin what my son was wearing, and that I would call her back later.

It was now time to take pictures, and my husband began snapping pictures. Joseph Marcus left to pick up his date. The doorbell rang and here came another beautiful young couple. They looked elegant. We took their pictures and, of course, I had to get in the picture with them. They left and moments later Marcus arrived with his date, Therese. They were a beautiful couple; Therese's dress was exquisite, and she was wearing a baby blue evening gown that was off the shoulders, with a shawl to match. Marcus was handsomely dressed in his white tux, with a black vest, white and black shoes, black gloves, and black sash scarf with white fringes. He topped it off a white cane, SHARP! Joseph Marcus and his date left for the prom.

The Prom: While at the prom the Senior Prom King and Queen was announced and next they announced the Senior Prince and Princess. A hush came over the crowd, everyone was anxious to know who would be the Senior Prince of 1999, the last prom of the decade. A voice shouted out "and the Senior Prince of Center High for 1999 is Joseph McCray." The crowd went crazy; Joseph McCray was voted Senior Prince of 1999. Joseph strode up to the front and received his Prince Sash, and took his dance with the Princess. All eyes were on them as they danced the Royal Dance. Joseph and his date, Therese, together danced the last dance of 1999. After the prom and dinner, they talked and laughed with friends, reminisced of old times, after all the festivities had ended. Joseph Marcus got behind the wheel, after waving and saying the last goodbye. He started the vehicle and began to take his date home, which was approximately an hour away.

After the Prom: My son and his date were traveling the highway home, thus ending the prom of 1999. Excited about all the events that took place, and with a smile on his face, he tried to remember everything that had happened that evening, not wanting to forget anything, wanting to hold on to every minute. Smiling to himself, Joseph Marcus began to feel his eyelids getting heavy. Suddenly, out of nowhere the white sports utility van, (the one that I thought was pretty big), began to swerve. Trying to bring the van back under control, Joseph Marcus realized there was a car right in front of him. Trying not to hit the car, he swerved again. Now the van was out of control. Joseph Marcus suddenly realized he couldn't bring it under control.

The Call: The phone rang once, then it rang again. I answered.

I heard the voice on the other end; it began, "Mrs. McCray..."

"Yes," I quickly glanced at the clock on my night table, it was 5:40 a.m. I heard a voice, a man's voice, he began, "Your son, Joseph..."

That's all I heard, I sat up straight, heart racing.

The man continued, "He's been in an accident."

Now I was on my feet, looking at my husband, saying, "Marcus has been in an accident."

I quickly said to the man, "Is he alright?"

Fear gripped my heart. For the second time in my life, fear had a hold on me.

The man continued, "He's conscious, he's lying on the ground. He gave me your number."

I really can't remember what else was said; he tried to tell me where they were. I heard him and understood him, I knew the location, but when I tried to repeat it, it all came out wrong. I heard myself saying, "Tell me again,"

The same thing happened. Again I asked the guy to repeat himself for the third time. I couldn't comprehend what was going on, I told the man to tell my husband, who was now fully awake from his sleep. I gave the phone to my husband. While he was talking to the guy, I was praying, and within minutes we were on our way out. I told my daughter what happened. I followed behind my husband out of the door. He was trying to calm my fears. Everything happened so fast. On our way to the accident site we received a phone call from our daughter letting us know they were taking Joseph Marcus to the hospital. Immediately, we turned around and headed in another direction, with my husband reassuring me. We drove on, my husband was deep in thought, as was I. We continued to pray. Suddenly, a peace came over me. I was no longer fearful, I told my husband that our son was going to be ok.

We arrived at the hospital; the ambulance had arrived only seconds before us. They were talking to Joseph Marcus while going into the hospital's emergency area. My husband went to where the ambulance was and I went in another direction. Standing at the emergency room window, the paramedic and my husband were coming to where I was, and the paramedic began to tell me what a good kid Joseph Marcus was. He was fine. Praise God!

Immediately, they began to work on him, ran every type of test possible. I then called home to let my daughter, Christine, know what was going on, which by this time everyone in the house was up and getting ready to come to the hospital. I told Christine to call my sister, Vanessa, and let her know what was going on, and for her and her husband to pray for their nephew. Around 7-7:30 a.m. We were able to see our son. We walked into the emergency room, looked at him, and knew how God had blessed him and how blessed we were. We began to thank GOD. I opened my mouth to pray. The word, "Father..." came out, then tears gushed out and ran down my cheeks uncontrollably. I looked at my son again with tears flowing. My husband began and ended the prayer. Tears continued to stream with uncontrolled sobbing, you see I was looking at a "miracle." When we came out of the emergency room, Joseph Marcus' best friends were already there. I let his friends know that he was o.k. Back into the emergency room I went and we were informed that other tests needed to be run on Joseph Marcus for the next two hours. We let our son know that we would be in the waiting area, and again we let him know how much we loved him, how blessed he was, and how blessed we were.

The Family: My husband and I left the hospital, knowing how blessed we were, we headed for a small restaurant only minutes away from the hospital. Around a half hour later we received a call on the cell phone; it was our kids letting us know that they were at the hospital. We told them where we were and in 10-15 minutes they arrived and we were all together. I will never forget how all the kids walked in one by one, each with their own serious face. They all wanted information. I opened my mouth, and the tears gushed out again. My husband had to tell them what happened. As I looked around the table everyone was silent. I believe they were having their own personal thoughts and saying their own personal prayer. I looked at my daughter, Christine, who had tears running down her cheeks, I looked at my son, Ken, who was tilting his head so the tears wouldn't fall, I looked at my stepson, who had a solemn look on his face. My husband had a reassuring look on his face. I was able to say to my family that God had his hand of Mercy on their brother, our son. My daughter-in-law asked about our oldest son, if he knew what had happened? I told her, "Not yet, but I will call his wife and let her know what is going on" (Terrance is in the Navy and was on deployment at the time).

We all left the restaurant, knowing we were a blessed family. We headed back to the hospital and they were still running tests; finally we were able to see him. The kids went in, one by one, to see their brother. It was now approximately 2-3:00 in the afternoon. All of the tests were run, and Joseph Marcus was now able to go to a hospital room. I looked again at my son and thanked God. I looked at the bruises and scars in his head, on the side of his face. His right eye was black on the outside and bloodshot on the inside, his left eye had blood spots on it. His shoulder was dislocated and I looked at the stitches on his right thigh. Yes, I looked at my son and, yes, I thanked God again and again. Joseph Marcus began to rest. The word was out and his friends now knew what happened. The phone calls were coming in from his friends, and, of course, Therese. They all had concerns but I had to reassure them that he was fine. His friends left the hospital, my kids left the hospital, and my husband and I left the hospital around 9:00 that evening.

Our day started with a phone call from a stranger. During this day, I believe each of us examined our relationship with each other. We knew how blessed we were. As for myself, I'd seen "God's Hand of Mercy."

God's Hand of Mercy: What actually occurred on May 16, 1999? When Joseph Marcus' rented utility van went out of control, the sports utility rolled over three to five times. Joseph Marcus was wearing his seat belt, but he was still thrown approximately thirty feet from the van. During that time he was unconscious, he landed on his face. When the sports van landed, it landed on its roof and the top was smashed in.

Again, I can say for myself, I've seen God's hand of Mercy. You know, God had his angels right there with Joseph Marcus. GOD already knew what was going to happen, and God placed His people there at the accident. He placed His people there at the appointed time. Again, I've seen God's hand of Mercy for myself.

How God uses strangers in our lives: The man who called

had seen everything; when he called he was calm and his voice was calm. He said, "Your son is conscious, and your son gave me the phone number." The man called the ambulance and police. Again, God's hand of Mercy.

God also placed someone else to see the accident. There was an off duty paramedic, yes, the off duty paramedic had seen the complete accident; he was able to talk to Joseph Marcus and keep him focused. Again, God's hand of Mercy.

The stranger, the paramedic, the ambulance, and the police arrived. Out of the two policemen, one was Joseph Marcus' football coach's wife. Again, God's hand of Mercy.

Remember the white sports utility van that I thought was pretty big. The last thing I said to Joseph Marcus was to "be careful." The Holy Spirit was leading me not to get the van or any other car. I passed this on to my husband and to my son. I told them how strongly I felt against this. The Holy Spirit will lead us and guide us. However, when He, the Spirit of truth, has come, He will guide you into all truth (John 16:13). Again God's hand of Mercy.

Later when Joseph Marcus was better he told us that when the vehicle began to swerve, he tried to gain control, but was unable to get control of it, and, struggling, he heard a voice, and the voice said, "Let go." "For He shall give His angels charge over you, to keep you in all your ways" (Psalm 91:11). Again, God's hand of Mercy.

When Joseph Marcus was released from the hospital, for the next week or so, his friends came over to encourage him. The house was full of young people. One thing I can say, teenagers will stick together and give their support.

You see, this is Joseph Marcus' testimony-- to let everyone

know what God has done for him. But it's also my testimony as well; you see I've seen God's hand of Mercy on my son and on my family. I've seen how God places His people everywhere and uses whomever He chooses. I told you earlier that the kids went in one by one to see their brother. Well, out of those, one of my kids prayed for their brother. Ken went in and prayed over his brother.

I know I am blessed, Joseph Marcus is blessed, and my family is blessed. We are all blessed.

To God be the Glory for ever and ever Amen.

I know for myself that right now, our son could well not be alive today. But because of God's Mercy he's here. I had to let my son know that it is because of God that he is here. That he is a miracle, God's miracle. That God has a work for Joseph Marcus to do, and it was not his time to go.

As I end this story of God's Hands of Mercy, I pray that you will be blessed by this story. You must know that there is no end with God. When we leave this life, those of us who have made Jesus our Lord and Savior will be present with the Lord.

Won't you make Him your Lord and Savior? Think about turning your life over to the one who created you and make Him your Lord and Savior. Won't you ask Jesus to come into your heart. Yes, now, right now.

The Bible says, "That if thou shall confess with thy mouth the Lord Jesus and shall believe in thine heart that God had raised Him from the dead thou shall be saved" (Romans 10:9).

"For whosoever shall call upon the name of the Lord shall be saved" (Romans 10:13).

Through the Eyes of a Baby

E arly one morning upon arising, I looked into a beautiful face that was staring and smiling at me. As I looked at this person I was overcome with joy. My heart was full and I thanked God for what He was doing in my life.

The joy of it all: "Joy." Exactly what is joy? Joy means: a condition or feeling of great pleasure or happiness, delight; a source or object of pleasure or satisfaction. The person that was smiling at me was my little granddaughter, Joycicana, and I realized that Jesus wants us to be filled with the joy that He has given us.

When my granddaughter visits she is dependent upon me to feed her, change her diapers, bathe her, dress her, and take care of her. She is dependent upon me to meet the needs in her life. She waits patiently to listen to what I have to say to her, and in her excitement she kicks her feet, smiles another smile, and tries to respond in her baby talk. As we both are actively aware of what is going on, I realize that we are bonding, an intimate relationship is being formed. I am actively playing a role and she is actively playing a role and while doing so, there is such a joy. If by chance I happen to be going through something, such as feeling down or whatever it may be, when she comes over I am no longer focused on my problems anymore--my focus, all my attention turns to her. I see her small face looking at me in amazement, and I realize that she is waiting for me to say something to her. She looks and she waits. I come to realize that she has recognized my voice. I had to speak to her many times for her to hear my voice and recognize my voice. Now when I speak she knows it is me.

Well, that is how we are supposed to be in Christ. We are to have our joy and our joy is to be in Christ Jesus. It amazes me, because as I ponder on this, I see how far from the mark I am. I thought I had joy, and I realize that my joy was really based on my emotions. Now, I am referring to me, Pam. I can only speak for myself. This may not be true for you, but as I write this I know it is true for me. What I thought I knew, I really did not know. Yes, you can sing the songs, such as "Joy, joy, God's great joy, joy, joy, down in my soul, sweet, beautiful joy, oh, joy in my soul," or "This joy that I have the world didn't give it and the world can't take it away." But as you sing, do you really know what you are singing? Yes, you can repeat scriptures, "Make my joy complete by being of the same mind, maintaining the same love ,united in spirit, intent on one purpose" (Philippians 2:2) or "Restore to me the joy of your salvation and sustain me with a willing spirit" (Psalm 52:12).

On this Christian journey it is a learning process. I thank the Holy Spirit for using a baby to show me the way. I truly believed that I had joy, but I see I did not have all the joy that the

Lord wants me to have. As I stated earlier, my joy was based on my emotions. The dictionary states that joy is a condition or feeling of great pleasure or happiness; delights. I can reflect on the times when things were not so right in my life, and now I can really see that I fooled myself into believing that I had joy. Oh, I would listen to Christian music, and try to make myself praise God, but now I ask myself, where was my joy? Perhaps I can encourage you as the Holy Spirit encouraged me. "But the fruit of the Spirit is love, joy, peace, patience, kindness, good-ness, faithfulness," (Galatians 5:22). Joy should be a part of my life every day, on all occasions, in season, out of season, daily, every morning, every afternoon, every evening, every day, all day. We should be experiencing God's joy on a daily basis, not when our emotions say, *ah, this is a good thing, go with the flow.* I have said on one occasion or another, "I am not feeling this today." Where was my joy? I pray that we can all experience the joy that God wants us to have, every day and all day. When we are awakened in the morning, we should see in our spirit, God just watching us, looking at us, and smiling at us. We should get up with joy. No matter how we feel or what we are going through, our joy should be there.

God wants us to be totally dependent on Him. He wants us to be excited about Him. He wants us to depend on Him to meet the needs in our lives. We should patiently wait and listen to what God has to say to us, and in our excitement we should kick our feet, clap our hands, do a Holy Spirit dance, sing a song and praise His name. Why? Because we know that He is smiling on us, and He's going to respond to us. As we wait, we are both actively aware of what is going on, Jesus and I.

In order for us to recognize God's voice, we have to bond with Him, we have to spend time alone with Him, and we have to have an intimate relationship with Him. We have to get in His Word, read His Word--read as if He is speaking to you only. We have to spend time alone with Him and, as we spend time alone with Him, we begin to hear His voice. Spending time alone with Him means talking to Him, and as He answers, we begin to recognize His voice.

As with Samuel, when he was a young boy, the first time God called him by name he did not recognize God's voice. But as he grew in the Lord, he began to recognize God's voice, and God used him mightily. But God kept calling Samuel, and with help from the high priest, he soon recognized God's voice, and he grew up and became obedient to what God told him to do.

As we read our Bible, God's word gives us God's character. The Bible tells us who God is, what He likes, dislikes, honors, and His promises to each of us. "In the beginning was the Word (Jesus) and the Word (Jesus) was with God and the Word (Jesus) was God, and the Word (Jesus) became flesh and dwelt among us and we saw His glory (John 1:1,14). We have to actively play a role. We have to seek after God, find out who He is and what His voice sounds like. He will answer us and He will reveal Himself to us if we diligently seek Him.

If, by chance, you are going through something and you feel drained, overwhelmed, or you are just tired of the situation, turn your focus, all of your attention to Jesus. God is looking at you in amazement and He is waiting for you to say something to Him. Explain your situation to Him. Look and wait expectantly for Him to answer you. Understand that if you have bonded with Christ, if you have been spending time alone in His presence, if you have been taking the time to get to know His character, His ways, then you will begin to recognize His voice. When He speaks to you, you will recognize His voice. "My sheep hear my voice, and I know them and they know me" (John 10:27). This comes from spending time alone with God.

Joy is not a superficial thing; joy is what God has given us to experience with Him. Our joy is complete in Christ Jesus. We should wake up with joy, no matter what is going on in our lives. We should see joy through the eyes of a baby, not act like a baby; because Christ does not want us to stay there. We are to grow spiritually from grace to grace. We should wait with excitement to hear from our Lord and Savior when He speaks to us. We should want to find out more about Him.

When we awaken in the morning, we should be able to smile and say, "Good morning, Holy Spirit, I see you smiling on me. All of our problems we should immediately give to Him, because He is waiting for us to be dependent upon Him. He does not want us to be bogged down with problems, having stressful days or restless nights. When it comes to finances, food, clothing, we should give all those cares to Him. His Word says that He will provide for all my needs. He wants to take care of us; all we have to do is joyfully let Him. With every problem that we have, He is waiting for us to bring all our cares and concerns to Him. He wants us to dwell in His presence and have joy.

As my baby granddaughter looks at me with a smile on her face, God wants us to look at Him with a smile on our faces. As my baby granddaughter is dependent upon me, God wants us to be dependent upon Him in all areas of our lives. As my baby granddaughter kicks excitedly at the sound of my voice, God wants us to be excited at the sound of His voice. As my baby granddaughter holds onto my finger so tight and won't let go, God wants us to hold onto Him so tight and not let go. As my baby granddaughter cries, God wants us to cry out to Him. As I pick up my baby granddaughter to comfort her, God wants to pick us up and comfort us. As I sing songs to my granddaughter, God want us to sing songs of praise to Him. As I protect the baby so that no harm comes to her, God watches over us and sees that no harm comes to us. As I watch my baby granddaughter peacefully sleep, God watches over us as we peacefully sleep.

Now I know what that song means, "Oh, the joy that I have the world did not give it to me and the world cannot take it away." You see this joy is freely given to and all we have to do is freely accept. My joy is in my Lord and Savior Jesus Christ, who lovingly wants all of me and not just part of me. He wants me to experience His joy, and through taking care of a baby, I get a glimpse of what true joy really is, and how I have not totally experienced all the joy that God wants me to experience. On my tear stained cheeks and with the humbleness of my heart, I pray that I will learn to awaken to joy, have joy during the day, during the night, and experience joy to the fullest. In my own weakness, I thought I had joy, only to realize that with me it was only an emotion. I pray that God will use me as a vessel that my mouth will be His mouthpiece, and my feet will be like hind feet. I had to spend time alone with God to recognize His voice and as He began to speak to me, I had to learn His voice and recognize His voice.

I can remember so clearly the first time He spoke to me; it was awesome, and at the same time He was answering my prayer. I had peace, I wiped away my tears, and I began to understand that this Christian journey is bigger than you or I. God had to prepare my heart to recognize His voice. My heart had to be prepared for what He wanted me to hear so clearly. One day God spoke to my Spirit. It was so very clear and all day I heard, "How will they hear without the word." This stayed with me all that day; it was so very clear. The next day, I got up with that in my mind, at work I was sharing with a sister in Christ, we pulled out the Bible, and came to Romans 10:14: "How will they hear without the preacher?" but God specifically spoke to me and said "the Word not Preacher." I know that my calling is getting God's Word out as He gives it to me. When God calls us to do something, I've found that things will come against us. For me, it's been a long journey of asking God questions, and not understanding all of the turmoil. I don't truly understand why some people go and some people come, and why some people speak against us. Yet I struggled to move forward. I've found myself becoming tired, not caring anymore, and wanting to give up on the promises of God. This morning, as I was driving to work, God put a picture of a baby in my mind and how I help take care of my granddaughter, the joy that she brings me, and then it was so clear. I spoke out loudly and said, "That's it, that's how God wants me to have complete joy in Him." At that moment it was all so very clear.

I have shared some things with you that I would have kept to myself; but being obedient to the leading of the Holy Spirit, I shared some of me with you. As I finish this section, I pray that your joy might be complete in Christ Jesus. That whatever God has called you to do you will move forward and complete. If it's a struggle, just keep moving. As I go through the things that I go through in the name of Jesus, now I can go through them with joy, full joy, complete joy, realizing that it is not an emotion, but it is a small deposit of what Christ has given me. "His master said to him, well done, good and faithful servant. You were faithful with a few things, I will put you in charge of many things; enter into the joy of the Lord" (Matthew 25:21). As I enter into the joy of the Lord, enter into what He is calling me to do, I do it with joy. I realize that God wants me and you to have complete joy in Him, joy every day, all day, not sometimes but all the time.

If you do not know Christ, I pray that you will accept Him as your Lord and Savior, experience His joy for yourself. Salvation is a free gift that He gives freely, He does not push Himself on anyone, but He does stand at the door of your heart. Accept Him. For those of you who want a more intimate relationship, I pray that you seek God with all your heart, and come to want to know more about Him. "Father, God we come before you, we come asking you to forgive us of our sins. Father, I pray that those who do not know you will want to know you and give their lives to you freely, and experience your complete joy. Father, I pray that those who begin seeking you will seek you with an earnest heart, and to spend time alone with you, and get to know you. Father, I pray that those who want your complete joy will realize that you freely give, and all we have to do is freely accept it and recognize that joy is not an emotion. Father, I ask that you prepare the people's hearts, and meet the needs in their lives. I pray that we all can experience your complete joy.

He Touched Me

It was an ordinary Saturday morning, nothing out of the ordinary, just a beautiful, gorgeous morning. My husband and I were sitting at the kitchen table talking and having coffee.

I was on my sixth day of fasting. I went to the kitchen table to read my scriptures for the day, but before I started reading, I decided to text my son some scriptures on healing. This led me to giving him the words that my mother gave me: "Always, put your faith, hope, and trust in the Lord." I wanted to be sure that this was correct and I did not want to add anything to it, so I went to get the Bible that my mom gave me where she had written those very words, and yes, the words were the same.

As I looked at the Bible that my mother had presented to me, it brought some tears as I remembered that the saying of those words was very precious to her and to me.

I went back to the kitchen table and turned to Psalms and began to read the Psalms on praise. I just wanted to praise the Lord and this led me to go to my secret place to praise the Lord.

Suddenly, an ordinary Saturday turned out to be an extraordinary Saturday morning. I stood in my secret place praising God. I lifted up my hands and said, "Lord, I surrender to you." I found myself asking Him to cleanse me and to use me. I got down on my knees and continued to praise Him. I started to feel a cleansing; I called out even more for the Lord to cleanse me.

Just then, I heard a still small voice, which was the Holy Spirit say, "Enter in with praise and thanksgiving." I continued to praise God and thank Him. I understood the scriptures that say; enter into His gates with thanksgiving and into his court with praise (Psalm 100:4).

I continued to praise and thank Him; again, I heard the Holy Spirit say, "Enter in." Again, I continued on with thanksgiving and praise. I heard myself say, "Lord I extol you." Then I said, "Lord, if You be lifted up You will draw all men to You" (John 12:32). I repeated this again, but this time it was like I said it with authority, like I fully understood what that meant. I spoke in tongues, still praising the Lord, and the Holy Spirit said to me, "Get ready." I continued to press on and suddenly, clearly, I heard the Holy Spirit say, "When you speak bring my people back to Me." Over and over he repeated this, "Bring My people back to Me." I heard myself repeating this over and over what He was saying to me. This went on for some time. Then I began to say, "Yes Lord, yes Lord."

But let me take a moment here and describe to you all that was going on. While the Holy Spirit was speaking to me, everything seemed as though it was going very fast.

While on my knees, I was crying uncontrollably, my body was shaking, and I kept repeating what the Lord was saying, but it seemed as if I could not say it fast enough. I kept trying to say it faster and faster, as the Lord kept saying to me, "Bring My people back to Me." It seemed as though it was a lot of noise all around me, and everything appeared as though it was happening very rapidly, and in the midst of it all, the Holy Spirit was telling me what to do in a still small voice. Everything was so fast; I was speaking very rapidly, trying to keep up with what the Holy Spirit was telling me to do. I finally heard myself say, "Yes, Lord, yes Lord, over and over again. By now, I am prostrate on my face on the floor saying, "Yes, Lord, I will bring Your people back to You. Yes Lord, yes Lord, I hear you, Lord." When I cried out to the Lord, it was though it was a bellowing cry being released from my inner being. It was so powerful!

Finally, still lying prostrate on the floor, but now I was taking it all in what the Holy Spirit had just instructed me to do and what I had just experienced. I just lay there on the floor in awe. My body was extremely tired, but yet on the inside I felt strong and powerful.

It seems as though the Holy Spirit took me by the hand and was leading me with baby steps. He was instructing me all the way. He told me to enter in with praise and thanksgiving, and he repeated this a second time, and when he spoke the third time, he said "Get ready." I could hear Him very clearly, with everything that was going on. He was leading and guiding me into the presence of the Lord. WOW!

What an anointing, awesome, miraculous time for me--a time I will never forget. How the Holy Spirit led me into the

Presence of the Lord and how I was given a specific instruction. This has never happened to me like this before.

I give God all the praise and all the glory for what He is doing in and through my life, and for what He is about to do. God knows! Praise God.

He's Worthy to Be Praised

"**P**raise the Lord! Praise the Lord, O my soul! While I live I will praise the Lord: I will sing praises to my God while I have my being" (Psalm 146:1-2).

Are you downtrodden, sad, rejected, alone, confused, misunderstood, angry, or ill? Have you had sleepless nights and restless days? Have your tears run down your face uncontrollably? Have you been through something, maybe now for weeks, months, or a year ago, and that same thing is still knocking on your door? Have you tried to be all you could to someone and found that doesn't work? Have you tried to protect someone from being hurt and only made matters worse? Have you loved someone with all your heart and found out that person does not love you the same way? Have you tried to be someone's savior and found out you need saving yourself, or have you tried to catch someone and found yourself falling? Have you tried to carry someone's burden and found yourself in sinking sand? Have you been lied to, talked about, or mistreated. Are you struggling with an addiction and think you have it under control? Have you walked away from the Lord and can't find your way back? Do you think that all is fine with you and you don't need the Lord? Do you say, "Hey, I am all right; all is good with me." If you can relate to one of the above, this story is for you.

Praise God! "For we have all become like one who is unclean, and all our righteousness (our best deeds of rightness and justice) is like filthy rags or a polluted garment" (Isaiah 64:6). While we were yet in weakness (powerless to help ourselves) at the fitting time Christ died for the ungodly" (Romans 5:6). But God shows and clearly proves His own love for us by the fact that while we were yet sinners Christ died for us (Romans 5:8).

Praise God! When we go through things, we must come to a place in which we totally depend on Jesus Christ, and it is sad to say, many Christians do not know how to get to that place. So we go on pretending. We go to church, we participate in ministry, and we act like we have it all together. How sad.

How do we get to the place in which we praise God for all that He has done for us? When we feel all alone, mistreated, and misunderstood. When we put on our Sunday face, you know the face that says all is well. I must interject here and encourage someone who needs to be lifted up. I must let you know that no matter what you are going through you are not alone, and for those of you who have no pain, no problems, and all is well within you, then you should encourage someone whose path you may cross.

I've learned that we go through ups and downs; we have hills to climb, and roads to cross. My heart goes out to those who are in chains, who are in bondage, who are bound, tied up, blinded by the enemy and do not know that Jesus Christ has already set them free. You don't have to go through life pretending; you are really missing out on God's precious plan for your life. Don't let the emptiness of life keep you from knowing who Jesus is. To know who Jesus Christ is, you must first have reverence for God. Reverence means a feeling of deep respect, love, awe and esteem.

First, we have to have respect for God, have a love for God, and be in awe of God. We have to have an intimate relationship with God. We are to rediscover who God is. Why? It is because He created us. What a privilege for the believer to be able to abide in our maker. Do you know what our first ministry is? Our first and most important ministry is to love God. If we can love God with all of our hearts, it becomes that much easier to love those who we believe have hurt us at one time or another. We can love our enemies and think nothing of it. Why? Because it is the love for God that rules us. In order to do this freely, we must have a desire to know God to meet with Him, to be obedient to His word.

Worship and praise go together; you cannot have one without the other. Worship acknowledges and praise is an act. We have to first acknowledge and then we act. How do we act? We praise God with our mouths, dancing, lifting our hands, and playing musical instruments. God is calling His people back to a true understanding of worship. It is time to return to God. We should not only speak of Him and about Him, but we should speak to Him, sing to Him, give Him glory, and give Him the honor and praise that He deserves. We are to rediscover who God is. Psalm 150 is the Hallelujah chorus, which states: "Praise the Lord! Praise God in His sanctuary; praise Him in the heavens of His power! Praise Him for His mighty acts; praise Him according to the abundance of His greatness! Praise Him with trumpet sound, praise Him with lute and harp! Praise Him with tambourine and dance; praise Him with stringed and wind instruments or flutes! Praise Him with resounding cymbals; praise Him with loud clashing cymbals! Let everything that has breath and every breath of life praise the Lord, Praise the Lord!" Hallelujah!"

God is to be praised by humans in His sanctuary, the temple. He is to be praised by angels in the mighty heavens. He is to be praised for His greatness and for the things He has done. He has created the universe, rescued His people and made them His own. He is to be praised with instruments, praised with singing, praised with dancing, praised with clapping of hands, and praised by our righteous actions. This is the ultimate purpose and fulfillment of all God's creatures, angels, and humans to unite in praising Him.

So, how does worship and praise go hand in hand? Worship is to revere and pay homage to God, the act of profound adoration, to give God the glory due to His name, to bow down before Him, drawing near to God and loving Him affectionately, as well as esteeming and respecting Him. Again, worship and praise is an action: first we acknowledge God, to know God, to know Him intimately, and then we praise Him. Praising God is an act, an act of expression.

Therefore, when we put these two things together, we are acting by acknowledging God and praising Him (which is an act) with our mouths we speak it or we do it. We are putting our faith into action. It's not just an outward appearance, for the Bible says we must worship Him in Spirit and Truth. We can praise Him with sincere hearts and in truth. "A time will come, however, indeed it is already here; when the true worshippers will worship the Father in Spirit and in Truth. For the Father is seeking just such people as these as His worshipers" (John 4:23). Remember that worship and praise is our first ministry. Only true worshipers can worship God. If you don't know Him nor know of Him, how then can you worship Him? What happens when we worship God? When we enter into His depth, we are convicted of sin, and are filled with the Holy Spirit. The Lord speaks to us, we fill our minds with Him, we bless Him, and God prepares our hearts.

In times of trouble, come before God with a song in your heart and praise on your lips, believe God and stand on the promises of God. Dance your dance, sing your song, sing to Him, talk to Him, acknowledge Him, and worship and praise Him. We serve an awesome God. Praise His mighty Name. Amen!

"Praise the Lord; Praise God in His sanctuary, praise Him in the heavens of His power! Praise Him for His mighty acts; praise Him according to the abundance of His greatness! Praise Him with trumpet sound; praise Him with lute and harp! Praise Him with tambourine and dance, praise Him with stringed and wind instruments or flutes! Praise Him with resounding cymbals; praise Him with loud clashing cymbals! Let everything that has breath and every breath of life praise the Lord! Praise the Lord! (Psalm 150)

By Faith

§

There comes a time in our lives when we have to take a deep heart-wrenching look at ourselves. We have to be honest with ourselves, and ask the question, "Am I doing all I can for my Lord and Savior, Jesus Christ?" As you ponder on this question, you have to be willing to see some areas in your life that God wants to change. If you or I profess to be a Christian, yet we are walking in the ways of the world, may I ask you, just who are we deceiving? When we say that we love the Lord and we live for the Lord, yet we have bitterness, unforgiving attitudes, anger, hatred, and strife in our hearts, who are we deceiving? When we quarrel among ourselves and with others who are we deceiving? When we speak badly about another person, who are we deceiving?

Jesus Christ is our perfect example; He showed us how we should live, how we could live a victorious life. Jesus Christ stated that, "I am the way the Truth and the Life." He chose us who are in Christ today, to be a light to a dark and dying world. Therefore, we have an obligation, a duty; we have a job to do. Jesus Christ was a humble man, a man full of compassion and love. He loved and he did not hold back His love from us. Our obligation is to be an example to others; to live a life worthy of our calling. We are God's spokespersons. We may be the closest person through which others might see Christ. Why, then, do we let the deceiver deceive us? "In the beginning was the Word, and the Word was with God, and the Word was God. The Word became flesh and dwelt among us, and we saw His Glory, glory as of the only begotten from the Father, full of grace and truth" (John 1:1,4).

It is because of Christ that we have our being. I have been questioned on who Christ is, what is the Trinity, why do I believe what I believe? I can sum it up very sweetly. I live and I have my being in Jesus Christ. One day I accepted and I asked Christ to come into my heart and live, to change me and transform me into what He wants me to be. I did this by "faith." Once I did this, I did not hear thunder clapping, or feel the earth being shaken. I was not looking for signs and wonders. I was looking for Jesus Christ. He came into my heart to live, and through His Word He opened up my eyes to wisdom, understanding, and knowledge. In His Word, God said, "Let us make man in our image, according to our likeness (Genesis 1:26).

The trinity is the Father, Son, and Holy Spirit. Jesus prayed to His Father. God acknowledged that Jesus was His Son in whom He was well pleased. Jesus stated, "I will ask the Father, and He will give you the Holy Spirit (comforter), that He may be with you forever" (John 14:16). I believe this by "faith," because I believe the Word of God.

Question as you read the history books; do you believe the

things that you read? Do you believe those things as truth and accept them as they are, not questioning or doubting? I read and believe my Bible, because in God's Word there's history. He has told us how the world began, what's going on now, and how it is going to end. I believe by "faith." I believe what I believe because of the precious blood of Jesus that He shed for me while He was on the cross. He was obedient to the Father, and obediently gave His life for mine. I believe by faith.

Let's take a look at the disciples, who were unlearned men--fishermen. Let's look at the transformation that took place in their lives after the Resurrection (Christ's death). They stood up before men and boldly preached the Gospel of Jesus Christ. They did not have a spirit of fear, but these men now had a spirit of power, love, and a sound mind. Ah, wait; let's take a look at Pam and the transformation in my life. Because of the blood that was shed for me, I see myself today as a soldier on the battleground for Christ. I have seen for myself how He has fought my battles for me--how He has performed in the life of my family. It was nothing that I did; it was all because of His mercy and grace. While He was hanging on the cross, He looked just over the land. He looked some 2000 years into the future, and He knew that the day was coming when my family and I were going to need Him like never before. He heard me crying out to Him like never before. He saw the tears that I would be shedding as I looked to my Master. He stayed, He stayed, and He stayed right there on the Cross.

I can hear Him say, "Pam don't you worry, I am here on the Cross for you and others like you. I see the need in your life. I want to give you a future and a hope." Oh, my sisters and brothers, I can hear Him so clearly saying, "I am on this cross for the remission of sins that each of you might have life and have it abundantly." While He was on the Cross, things happened that never happened before. Oh, I tell you there was a spiritual war that was going on right then and there. My Bible tells me that from 12:00 p.m. to 3:00 p.m. the sun was unable to let her violet rays flow, the earth was covered with darkness, scriptures were being fulfilled that day. What the Bible had stated was coming to pass.

Do I believe? I believe by "faith." You see, because of my Lord and Savior Jesus Christ, the Resurrection Power, and His love for my family and me. I can only pray, 'Jesus change me.' I don't want to be the same. I know who I am in Christ Jesus and I have a destiny to fulfill. It grieves my heart to soreness because some are not aware of what actually happened on the cross. It is now taken so lightly, as if it is of no importance. Because Jesus was obedient to the cross, he was the lamb sacrificed for your sins and mine and because of this we now have a future with Jesus Christ. He has given us a free gift, but, sad to say, there are so many out there who do not accept the gift--the gift of salvation.

We have a future, when these old bodies of ours die, we will be in the presence of the Lord. There will be no more tears, no more pain, no more hatred, no more sickness, no more heartache, no more disappointment, no more regrets, and no more crippling disease in the body or in the mind, no more death and no mourning. All things will be made new. We will see our Lord and Savior, Jesus Christ, the Alpha and Omega, the beginning and the end, we will behold His glory, and we will see His face. We will see our loved ones who have gone on before us. The city we will live in has twelve gates, with twelve angles at the gates, and our names written in the Lamb's Book of Life. May I ask you, will your name be there? It is time my sisters and brothers for us to look to Jesus to change us; to transform us into what He wants us to be. We can no longer deceive others, for we are only deceiving ourselves. If you need a touch, a personal touch from Jesus Christ Himself, all you have to do is completely cast all your cares on Him. There are some who are sick in their bodies and minds. There are some that need help in their finances and need a job. There are some that are caught up and have a monkey on their back. This monkey could be of any size, shape or form, and you just can't shake it. Give it to God. There are some who are caught up in drugs, alcohol, and pills. There are some in wrong relationships, who have been abused and don't know how to forgive and love. There are some who lie, cheat, and steal--some who gamble, and play the lottery. There are some who have poor self-esteem about themselves. There are some who don't feel loved, some feel friendless, and some with no self-control. There are some who curse with their mouths and turn around and pray in the name of Jesus. Finally, there are some who do not believe in Jesus Christ.

In this day and time, we do not have to stay where we are right now. There comes a time in our lives when we have to truly trust God and believe His Word. For those of you who say you are Christians and don't believe in the work of Jesus Christ, or that He hung on Calvary's cross for your sins, then I implore each of you to truly walk in the ways of the Lord. If you are a Christian, yet you are still walking in the ways of the world, I ask you to take a look at the Power of the Cross. Jesus Christ outwitted the enemy's tactics; you are free in Christ Jesus. When you profess to be a Christian and walk in the ways of the world, other people see you as a hypocrite. A hypocrite is a person who has two faces and acts one way or another, depending on the circumstances. Please do not look at what Jesus did on the Cross and make nothing of it.

If you need a transformation, ask Him to change your heart. We are to live upright lives. Whatever we do in our flesh we represent Christ. If you feel spiritually sick, then get back in the Word, read God's Word anew, and ask the Holy Spirit to give you a new hunger to learn more about God and His will for your life. If you feel lonely, unloved, look at the Cross and what Jesus did for you, because God gave His only begotten Son for us. That's love.

If you don't know Christ and you want to know Him, The Bible says that "if you confess with your mouth the Lord Jesus and believe in your heart that God has raised Him from the dead, you will be saved" (Romans 10: 9). Ask Him to come into your heart and live and transform your life. If we just take a look at everything that is going on around us, look at the turmoil and chaos that the world is in. Better yet, just look at what's going on in and around you. It is time for each of us to say, *Lord, here I am, use me.* We have to be willing to acknowledge that some things in our lives need to be changed. Willing means surrendering our will over to the Lord, acknowledging that He is directing us, He is ordering our steps.

What is God's will for your life? Good question. First, it is God's will for us to accept Him as our Lord and Savior, then to fully trust Him with our lives. If we don't know how to live a life worthy of our calling, then God's Word tells us exactly how we should live. As Christians we are to present ourselves to God (becoming a sacrifice that is living, holy and pleasing to God) and receive transformation by a renewed mind (discovers and displays the will of God). "I beseech you, therefore, brethren, by the mercies of God, that you present your bodies a living sacrifice, holy, acceptable to God, which is your reasonable service. And do not be conformed to this world, but be transformed by the renewing of your mind, that you may prove what is that good and acceptable and perfect will of God" (Romans 12:12). Transform means to change forms. In the New Testament, this word is used to describe an inward renewal of our minds through which our inner spirit is changed into the likeness of Christ. As our Christian life progresses, we should gradually notice that our thought life is being changed from Christ less to Christ like. Transformation does not happen overnight. Our regeneration is instantaneous, but our transformation is continuous. We are conformed to Christ's image gradually as we spend time in intimate fellowship with Him. May I repeat again and again? We are not perfect, but we strive to become better—not being complacent or comfortable with our spiritual lives. But to continuously go before the Lord and ask Him to change us. It's a process.

We all have something in our lives that needs to be transformed. But we have to realize that in our own strength we can do nothing. However, through Christ Jesus we can do all things. If you are being challenged in your bodies, I pray that you will go before the throne of grace and ask God to strengthen and heal your body, give you direction, instructions, and then you wait and listen to what He says. Hold on to the promises of God. Have "faith" in God, He wants you to come to Him. We need a transformation. We represent Him.

For those who do not have a personal relationship with the Lord, may I say, you are truly missing out on life. I know you think you've got it made, you have it all together, and you think everything that you have, you've done on your own, but you haven't.

Jesus Christ is our perfect example; He showed us how we should live, how we could live a victorious life. Jesus Christ stated that, "I am the way the Truth and the Life." He chose us who are in Christ today, to be a light to a dark and dying world. Therefore, we have an obligation, a duty; we have a job to do. Jesus Christ was a humbled man, a man full of compassion and love, He loved and he did not hold back His love for us. Our obligation is to be an example to others--to live a life worthy of our calling. We are God's spokespersons. We may be the closest person through which others might see Christ. Why, then, do we let the deceiver deceive us? "In the beginning was the Word, and the Word was with God, and the Word was God. The Word became flesh and dwelt among us, and we saw His Glory, glory as of the only begotten from the Father, full of grace and truth" (John 1:1, 4).

I'm Free in Thee

As the eagle soars high in the sky, my Spirit dances before thee. I'm free, free to dance, free to sing, free to give praises unto thee. My Spirit is free, free in Thee.

It is He who has made us and not we ourselves, we are His people and the sheep of His pasture, I'm free, free to praise Thee.

Let us not forget all of His benefits, who forgives all of our sins; I'm free, free to praise thee.

Because of His loving kindness and faithfulness; I'm free, free to praise thee.

Through the tears and through the pain; I'm free, free to praise thee.

When the storms are raging in and there seems to be no end, I'm free, free to praise Thee.

Through good times and bad times; I'm free, free to praise Thee.

From the early morning dew to the lonely sleepless nights; I'm free, free to praise Thee.

Through the disillusionment and confusion; I'm free, free to praise Thee.

When my heart is broken and wounded within me; I'm free, free to praise Thee.

With a song in my heart and a dance in my step; I'm free, free to praise Thee.

With every trial and tribulation; I'm free, free to praise Thee.

From the rising of the sun until its going down; I will praise Thee.

No man has a hold on me: I am not bound, I am not chained, there are no shackles on me, I'm free, free to dance, free to sing, free to give praises unto Thee; I will praise Thee.

No oppression, depression, or misconception can stop me; I will praise Thee.

Because of your mercy and because of your grace, I will praise Thee.

When rivers of water run down from my eyes, when I cry out with my whole heart, when I cry out to You; I will praise Thee.

When my enemies rise up against me, I will lift up my eyes to the hills, from whence cometh my help, and Your right hand will save me; Yes, I will praise Thee.

When words of hatred roll down my way, I will praise Thee.

When I don't understand what's going on in my life, but I know who holds my life in His hands; I will praise Thee.

From the rising of the sun until it's going down, I will praise Thee.

I am not bound, I am not chained, there are no shackles on me, no one has a hold on me. I'm free, free to dance, free to sing, free to give praises unto thee. My Spirit is free, free in Thee. Yes I will, I will praise Thee!

Woman of Valor

I am a woman, a Woman of Valor
It's not me you see but He who is in me.

So don't look at me and be surprised
When you see me take a stand and rise
It's not me you see but He who is in me.

So, when I boldly open my mouth and speak
And you begin to feel feeble-kneed and weak
It's not me who speaks but He who is in me

So, when I walk the walk
You know what I am talking about
Those brave walks that lead me onto the unknown path;
It's not me who walks but He who is leading me
He who is in me.

So, when you try to break me down
With your words and a frown
Always remember, I cannot be bound down;
It's not me who you try to break down
But He who is in me

I am a woman, a Woman of Valor
A courageous and brave woman
A woman of beauty, dignity and strength
I move forward in humility
Trusting and having hope within me

So, don't look at me and be surprised
When you see me rise
It's not me you see but He who is in me!

A Mother's Day Poem

The Lord is my shepherd I shall not want

Because of Mother's loving touch we hurdle danger bumps
Bruises we use as excuses for hugs and kisses

A gentle push in the right direction, plus bundles of affection
Showing love you have it perfected

She's the treasure in the trunk and the ice for my lumps

If I forget to pray, she has me covered that day

In a world of hurt she encourages growth spurts

No matter what I say, I thank God for your grace

Dear Mother,
God bless you on your day
May the Lord send many your way!

By Joel Kenneth McCray

How I Love Thee

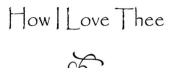

Oh, how I love Thee, to be in the presence of Thee,
To feel Your touch of love, the love that draws me to Thee.

Oh, how I love Thee, to be in the presence of Thee
To feel your warm smile and see You smiling at me.

Oh, how I love Thee, to be in the presence of Thee
To feel You holding me and drawing me closer to Thee

Oh, how I love Thee, to be in the presence of Thee
To see Your Glory and the brilliant light around Thee
That makes me humbly bow down to Thee

Oh, how I love Thee, to be in the presence of Thee
Knowing that you care for me
and for putting a song in my heart for Thee

Pamela McCray

Oh, how I love Thee, to be in the presence of Thee
That when troubles come my way, thee lifts and covers me.

Oh, how I love Thee, to be in the presence of Thee
with all of me, to love Thee, and know that You love me.

Oh, the love of Jesus
The love that lifted me
Oh, how I love Thee, to be in the presence of Thee

High in the Sky

I can fly high, high in the sky

I can fly into the eye of the storm,
I can fly in the sunlight, the moonlight, and in the starlight,
And come out knowing that everything is alright.

There are things that I must achieve
So, I spread my wings and soar, soar into the unknown.

As I spread my wings and fly, I can't be afraid of the unknown
because I know to whom I belong.

With the wind as my guide, and as I continue to glide,
I look over my past and I see that I must go higher
I look over the present and still I must go higher
I continue to fly, looking at my future
and I see, I must go even higher.

Pamela McCray

I can fly high, high into the sky,
Seeing, doing, believing, and touching other lives.

As my destiny calls me, I must spread my wings
And fly high, high, high into the sky.

Son

As the eagle spreads her wings
And flies high and alone

As the eagle flies in the
Brightness of the sky
I think of you and the days gone by

Your smile and laughter
brightens up my day

So spread your wings
and let the wind be your guide

Soar like an eagle
And fly high and alone

Let the Lord guide you in all
of your thoughts and all of your ways

And in the coming days
Let the Lord have His way

Always strive to do your best
and never ever settle for less.

Daughter

As the rainbow shines after the rain
As the butterfly flies, so sweet and light

As the sun burns so bright
I think of you and know
That everything is alright

I've seen you grow from short to tall
and only taken a few falls.

I see the tenderness in your eyes
I see a crown of beauty on your head
I see a smile on your face
Now it's time for you to join the race

Don't settle for outward appearance
Go deep inside yourself
Never settle for less
Always strive to do your best

The Lord blessed me
when He gave me you.

Sister

As the birds sing
as the butterfly flutters by
so does time
there goes the time

Times that sisters share
time to laugh, time to care, time to cry
time to bear one another's burdens
time to pray for each other
there goes the time

Time that you and I have shared
the good times and bad times
the sorrowful and glad times
there goes the time

Pamela McCray

Time that sisters share
time in laughter
time in tears and
time in pain
there goes the time

As the birds sing
as the butterfly flutters by
so does time
there goes the time.

Mama

Bella was home alone and sitting at her kitchen table in deep thought, when she heard someone knocking on the door. Bella slowly gets up from the table and heads to the door. "Who is it?" It's me, Tess. Bella takes a deep sigh, puts a smile on her face, and opens the door.

"Hi Tess."

"Hi Bella."

Bella asks Tess, "What are you doing over here, it's Saturday and nine o'clock in the morning?"

Tess looks at Bella, and says, "Bella, I don't know what you are going through, but this morning you were heavy on my heart and mind, and the Holy Spirit told me to come and see about you. You are my best friend, and we have been through a lot together. What's going on girl? You look troubled.

Bella says, "Come on in the kitchen, and I will pour you a cup of coffee."

Bella opens the cabinet and gets Tess a coffee cup, and slowly pours Tess coffee. Tess sees that Bella's hand is shaking.

Bella drops the coffee cup and the coffee spills all over the counter top and onto the floor. Bella is crying and she begins to tell Tess what just happened the night before.

Bella went to the hospital to see her mother, and she received a bad report.

She says, "The doctors told me that Mama was not going to make it, that they had done all they could do for her, and it was nothing else they could do. She's not in any pain; they have her on Morphine. She looks so tired. She says she's ready to see Jesus. I love my mama, I can't lose her. I can't lose her, what am I going to do without my mama?"

Tess grabs Bella, and tells her, "Girl, I am here for you, I will stay by your side." They both begin to cry together.

Tess lets Bella cry and talk, Bella says, "It was hard last night; I just sat there and looked at my mama and held her hand. She was in and out, but when she was aware of what was going on and who was around her, she told them that Jesus loved them and to be strong. She says she is going to a better place where there is no more crying. But when she talks about Jesus, her face brightens up, and she has the biggest and prettiest smile on her face. She's not looking at us, but she is looking toward heaven, and she smiles."

Bella tells Tess, "My siblings and I—we are aware of what's going on, but Tess it is just so hard. I love my mama. I can't make it without her. She keeps telling us to love one another, to be better towards each other, to take care of each other, and to keep the family together and strong. She says we can do it. She tells us not to let anyone come in and tear the family apart--for our spouses, sisters-in-law, and brothers-in-law to all stay strong. We can make a difference, to stop all the backbiting, talking about folks, and get along and just be nice to one another because time is too short for all that foolishness. If someone don't like you, they just don't like you and it ain't nothing you can do about it. You just pray for that person and turn them over to the Lord. But you always do what is right, no matter what that person does to you." Now, Tess, mama was about to pass to the other side, yet she was trying to get her family together in her last hours. What am I going to do without that wisdom? She is so strong. I need my mama! You know, Sometimes I have regrets, because my husband used to try to keep me from my mama. It bothered him that we were so close. But he knew that when we were dating. Go figure! But my mama sat him down one day and talked to him. I don't know what she said, all I know is that he changed after that. It didn't bother him that we were so close. To this day, I don't know what she said to him.

"But you know, Tess, I know I have to be strong. But one thing I know for sure, is that I will not pretend, I will never pretend to be someone that I am not. People like that, you know, when you pretend, that makes them feel better. But my mama always told us, 'Be yourself, just let the Lord lead you. If you do well, people gonna talk about you, if you do bad, guess what, people gonna talk about you. So just be yourself and let them talk. Don't try to please people, just try to please God.' See Tess, all that wisdom, I am going to miss that.

"But you know what else, Tess, last night my mama prayed for us. She prayed over each of her kids, over the family, finances, strength, and for all of us to have a closer walk with the Lord. She told us all that she loved us. Then she smiled that pretty big smile again, and said, 'I see Jesus.'

Bella was crying uncontrollably. "Mama is gone, Tess, she is gone. That's why the Lord sent you over here, He knew I needed you. I didn't call you, because I couldn't. I just needed to be alone. I am sorry for not calling you. I know you loved Mama too."

Tess said, "It's okay, Bella, girl; I understand. But what's important now is that I am here for you and your family." "Just remember what your mama told you: be yourself, you don't have to be strong for anyone--you just lean on and depend on Jesus. He is the one that can carry you through this. He is the one that can comfort you. It's going to take time, Bella, but with time Jesus will carry you through this. You just trust in the Lord when the tears come, and, believe me, they will come. You just let them flow. There will be times when you won't want to talk to anyone; that's okay too. There will be days when you feel like you are going through the motions; that's fine, too. There will be times when you want to question God and ask Him why; that's fine, too. You will have some sleepless nights and some restless days, but just trust in Him. Take all of your cares and concerns to Him. Just trust Him. On your best day, trust in Him; on your worst day, trust in Him. That's how you will make it, by trusting in the Lord.

"Oh Bella, girl, go ahead and shed your tears. Go ahead and let your heart be heavy now, go ahead and feel the pain, go ahead and ask God why. Shed your tears, Bella, let the anguish flow, and release that pain into the atmosphere. It's alright, Bella, I am here with you, and Jesus is here with you, He will never leave you or forsake you. He heals the broken-hearted and binds up their wounds (Psalm 147:3).

If you've lost a loved one, then the following poem is for you, because we are all someone's child.

This Child of Mine

To you I'll give a child of mine
To love, nurture, and cherish,
until it's the end of their time

Now I've looked up and down and
all around for someone to love this child of mine.

Upon my searching, I saw your heart, and knew you'd be the one
to play that important, perfect part--to connect heart to heart
with this child of mine,
until it's the end of their time

Now when this child of mine strays away from what you say,
and strays away from what you have taught them,
just remember, to still love this child of mine--
to go into your secret place and pray for this child of mine
until it's the end of their time

Pamela McCray

Be gentle, be kind, to this child of mine

Teach him or her, nurture him or her, and mostly love him or
her,
this child of mine, until it's the end of their time
and who knows the time?

And when it's the end of their time
I'll remember how you loved
and cherished this child of mine

Go ahead, and shed your tears, for this child of mine
but just remember, I had to search all around for you
to love this child of mine, that's when I saw your heart
and knew you'd be the one to play that important, perfect part,
to connect heart to heart with this child of mine
until it's the end of their time

Thank you for taking care of this child of mine
until it's the end of their time
and who knows the time?

Believe

Believe this is your time, your year, your now, your 'immediately', 'your suddenly', just believe.

The word *believe* has been in my mind and spirit for over a year now; so let me share with you what God has taught me and is still teaching me about the word *believe*. First you must believe that all things are possible. Your situation and circumstance may be saying something else to you, but believe that what you are going through right now is only for a season. That it is within your power to shorten the season that you are in right now. How can you do that?

Believe that God is a Big God, and He is bigger than your problems, situation, or circumstance. He can handle what you are going through; give your problem over to the Lord.

My calling is to exhort and encourage God's people by speaking what He says. When I was called many years ago; I heard the Spirit of God say, "How will they hear without the word?" I heard this over and over for one and a half days. How will they hear without the Word? I was just getting back into church at this time, so I didn't know that was the Holy Spirit speaking to me at the time; and I certainly did not know how to find where the scriptures were or even what it meant. But God had a person in my life, and as I shared with her what was going on, she said, "Let's look and see what it says in the Bible." We came across Romans 10:14 "How then shall they call on Him in whom they have not *believed*?" And how shall they *believe* in Him of whom they have not heard?"

Then it goes on to say, "How will they hear without a preacher." But God spoke to me and said "How will they hear without the Word." That was over eighteen years ago.

The meaning of *believe:* To have confidence in the truth, the existence, or the reliability of something although without absolute proof the one is right in doing so; only if one believes in something can one act purposefully.

I tell you the truth, I was baptized and received Christ when I was a child, and walked away from the church. When I went back to church, I didn't know anything; I didn't even know who God really was. I am just being truthful. At one evening service a visiting minister came to our church and was giving the sermon, and at the end of his sermon, (It is still very clear to me this day), he said, "Lift up your hands and tell God you love Him." I looked all around, people were raising their hands and telling God they loved Him. I raised my hands, looked toward heaven, and said, "God, I don't even know you, so how can I say I love you?" (The thought of not truly knowing Him at that time, blows my mind. I am just being honest). Wow! That was the beginning for me. My heart was ready. I didn't know what I was saying, but it was the truth. You see, God wants us to know Him and have a personal relationship with Him. We have to be ready to receive from Him. That was my beginning.

Afterward, God began to deal with me in a way that I had to learn His character and who He was. I began to read my Bible, and began to experience God's words. His words became alive to me. I began to get understanding, wisdom, and knowledge of what He was saying. Things began to change for me; my whole world was turned inside out. I started to go through and I mean go through some things. That is where and how I learned to depend on God. I had to! I could not have made it without Him. As I stayed in His Word, went to church, and cried throughout those times, He was working in me. I didn't know it; the only thing I was feeling was pain." My situation was painful, hurtful, and depressing; it knocked the breath out of me, literally. Who could I talk to; who would understand? I didn't know what to do. So I cried and I cried, and I cried out to God. My pain was so painful that on a Saturday morning I was up and in the shower at 6:00 a.m. I remember saying to myself, "It's going to be a long day, what am I to do?" and again the tears came, and again I cried and cried. Throughout the day I cried. The pain was unbearable. Thank God, thank God, thank God, that He kept me. I took comfort and depended on God like never before. I took comfort in God's Word and in God. I had to; I was at wit's end, at the end of my rope. I had to look to Him for strength and help. Without Him, I tell you I could not have made it! But it was time, it was time to know Him, to let Him love on me during my painful time.

I started praying, praying the best way I knew how at that time. I began reciting scriptures. I talked to God and during that painful, hurtful time, He comforted me in a way you would not believe. I finally knew God's love for me, and I was able, now really able to say, "Lord I love you." Yes, through all of that, I was able to say with a heart full of love for the Lord. "Lord, I love you."

Who would have thought that I had to go through such a painful situation or circumstance, to be able to say, "Lord, I love You"? I can tell you today, I thank God, and I would not change what I went through. I thank Him that I went through that. If not, I would not be who I am today, and I can honestly say, "Lord, I love you." I can say to you, "I love Him, I love Him, yes, I love Him." If I had not gone through my situation, my problem, I would be just going through life, not having a purpose, being self-dependent instead of being dependent on God. Yes, I love Him. Yes, I can say before you, through it all, I am still here. God had to do a work in me. I felt like I was being crushed, but a beautiful fragrance was being presented before the Lord. I was becoming transformed into my beginning of what He wanted for me. I was becoming a new creature in Christ Jesus. I was His and He was mine.

Where are you at? Do you need Jesus? Do you need to know His love for you, His purpose for your life? Do you need to experience His joy? Is your hope lost? What are you going through? Are you having sleepless nights, do you hear the tears dropping on your pillow at night? Do you feel hopeless and helpless? Are you just stumbling through life? Where are you at? Are people treating you wrong, being disrespectful, not accepting your position. Are you having difficulty on the job, kids not acting right, bills need to be paid, not enough food on the table, lost a loved one? Are you being treated badly by the one you love? All is not lost. There is hope and His name is Jesus. Jesus Christ, the anointed one. Where are you at?

I declare this day; you can come out of your situation, your circumstance, your problem. How? Give it to Jesus. Believe nothing is impossible for God. Nothing is too big for Him. Let me encourage you this day; let me help you this day. Oh, I know, I know, I know, you're at wits end. Believe me when I say, that's a good place to be in, because you are ready to receive. Give your problems over to the Lord--don't resist. Give it to Him. Let God help you. He is willing, ready, and able. Cry out to Him. This is your now, this is your time, your season, this is your now.

For those who are afraid to do what God has called you to do, now is the time for you to move and be obedient to what He is calling you to do. Believe that you can do all things through Christ who strengthens you. You can't do it in your own strength, but in Christ you can.

Get up! Move! Become what God wants you to become; do what He is calling you to do. I am here to encourage you, exhort you, to help you hear what He is saying. How will they hear without the Word? This is your time; you know what you are supposed to be doing. You know what God has called you to do. You know what He is telling you to do. You have a clue; you are not clueless. He may be saying, get up, move forward, move from the situation you are in--only you know what situation, circumstance, or problem you are in. Is it burdening you, is it bringing you down, making you feel lifeless, making you stressed out, confused, and leaving you empty?

Do you feel like I felt many years ago, when I was consumed by my problem, not knowing what to do or who to talk to? Is your situation painful, hurtful, and depressing? Do you feel like the breath was knocked out of you? Is your pain unbearable?

Believe God is able, believe He can work through you and in you. What are you afraid of? I declare now, you do not have a spirit of fear, but of power, love, and a strong mind. You are stronger than you think.

Believe that you can accomplish and do what He has called you to do; believe He can work through you, believe. He has a purpose and plan for your life: believe that every need is met, believe your finances are met, believe your health is good and you are healed from the top of your head to the soles of your feet. Believe.

Now, by believing, you have to put some action (faith) to your trust. How? Get up, move, get your Bible and declare God's Word over your family, finances, health, purpose, creative ideas, and relationships. Believe He is able. Believe when you speak His Word aloud and declare His words over your life that He is able. Believe! Believe that son, daughter, mother, father, sister, brother, husband, wife is saved and coming back to the Lord. Believe your household is saved. Believe!

Now, if you are reading this and want to accept Jesus Christ as your Lord and Savior, say: "Lord, I admit I am a sinner and need your forgiveness. I confess with my mouth and believe in my heart that Jesus was raised from the dead. Come into my life and help me live a life that pleases you. Amen!"

Now, if you have prayed this prayer, get into a Bible teaching church, and start reading your Bible, start in the Book of John. Let people know that you have accepted Jesus Christ as your Lord and Savior. Praise God!

Believe this is your season, your time, and your right now. Believe!

Just Believe

elieve you can, believe in the Lord. Only if one believes
in something, can one act purposefully. Believe in your
purpose-driven life, believe in your destiny, believe, deep
within yourself, within your inner being. Because now is the
time, this is the time, this is your time to believe. Just Believe!

Believe this is your season, your time; believe that with the
lives you touch, you can make a difference. Just Believe.

Believe and know you're right in believing, because the
time is at hand when you'll say this is it, this is my time. It's
time to believe you can, believe in your destiny, believe in your
purpose, believe and trust in the Lord, believe it's your time.
Just Believe!

Believe that you can go where you haven't gone before,
believe you can touch what you never touched before, believe
you can see what you haven't seen before, and believe you can
hear what you never heard before. Just Believe!

Believe you can, believe in yourself. Believe in the Lord
who is directing and ordering your footsteps. Go ahead,

believe that you can, not because I told you so, but believe that you can. Believe and trust in the Lord. Just Believe!

No matter what you might be going through, or have been through, or have yet to go through, just believe that you can overcome the obstacles in your path. Be strong, be courageous, and move forward, not in your own strength, but in the power of the Lord. Let the Lord lead you and guide you. As you believe in yourself, also believe in Him. He is able to help you on your journey to do things that you never thought or imagined you could do. Remember always, you have a divine destiny and you must make up in your mind and heart that no man or anything will stop you from the journey that you must take. So Believe! Believe that you can. Just Believe!

Believe you can, believe in the Lord. Only if one believes in something can one act purposefully. Believe in your purpose-driven life, believe in your destiny, believe, deep within yourself, your inner being. Because now is the time, this is the time, this is your time to believe, this is your season. Just Believe!

Oh No, Not Again!

I wrote earlier in the manuscript about the second auto accident in the family. This time it was my son, Ken, who was struck by a car that was fleeing from law enforcement. He ended up having hand surgery as well as hip surgery. It took him a very long time to heal. Below are some scriptures God gave me specifically for Ken during that period.

The Blessing:

I know the plans that I have for you, says the Lord, plans of good and not evil, plans to give you a future and hope (Jeremiah 29:11).

This is the plan that God has for Ken's life. Ken is still here, praise God. Yes, he is banged up, bruised up, and has rods and screws going through his body. But He is still here.

Psalm 91 is a psalm of trust:

He who dwells in the secret place of the Most High shall abide under the shadow of the Almighty. I will say of the Lord, "He is my refuge and my fortress; My God, in Him I will trust."

Surely, He shall deliver Ken from the snare of the fowler And from the perilous pestilence. He shall cover Ken with His feathers, And under His wings Ken shall take refuge.

His truth shall be Ken's shield and buckler. Ken shall not be afraid of the terror by night, nor of the arrow that flies by day, nor of the pestilence that walks in darkness, nor of the destruction that lays waste at noonday.

A thousand may fall at Ken's side, and ten thousand at Ken's right hand; But it shall not come near Ken. Only with Ken's eyes shall Ken look, and see the reward of the wicked.

Because Ken has made the Lord, who is Ken's refuge, even the Most High, Ken's dwelling place, no evil shall befall Ken, nor shall any plague come near Ken's dwelling; For He shall give His angels charge over him, to keep him in all his ways.

In their hands they shall bear Ken up, lest he dash his foot against a stone. Ken shall tread upon the lion and the cobra. The young lion and the serpent he shall trample underfoot.

Because Ken has set his love upon Me, therefore I will deliver him; I will set Ken on high, because he has known My name.

Ken shall call upon me, and I will answer him; I will be with him in trouble; I will deliver him and honor Ken, with long life I will satisfy him and show him my salvation.

To God be the glory forever and ever! Amen

Where Are They Now?

L ord, where are they, where are they now?! Where are the ones that you have given me, the ones you have given me to care for and to love? Where are they, Lord? Where are the children! Where are they? They run, they run here and there, searching, looking, trying to find that one thing or that one person who they believe can give them pleasure, make them happy-- someone who can complete the void in their lives.

They are looking, they are searching, and they are being deceived along the way. What can I do, what can I say? Is there anything I can do or say that will make a difference? I am crying for them, Lord Jesus, to come back home--to come back to where they belong. Come back!

Look, Father, Look at them.

Look at Sue and Jimmy. Father, look at them, they are running, running, running, trying to get away, trying to get away from the hurt and the pain that has been caused by alcohol and drugs.

Let's look at Sue. It all started when Sue's father abandoned her and her mother. She kept this inside her but she always felt that it was her fault that her father left. At a young age, she began to feel like something was wrong with her, and that she had done something wrong. She never felt like she belonged and she never felt good enough. Throughout her life she struggled and she went looking for love in all the wrong places. She was confused and she began to run. She ran right into the arms of this boy and that boy and, along the way, she ran into the arms of drugs.

Look at the lady who has five kids by five different men. Father, look at the girl or boy who is being molested in the home. Father, look at the girl or boy who is being physically and verbally abused. Father, look at the mother who is being physically and verbally abused in the home.

Look, look Father at the boy or girl who ran away from home, trying to get away. Father, look at the mother who has left home and left her children, trying to get away.

Look Father, look at the girl who had an abortion; she carries the guilt, shame, and pain with her. Look at her, Father, look.

Father, look, look, at the young girl and boy who have to take care of their mother, who is on drugs. Can you see them? Father, look at the little boy and girl who have to take care of themselves and fend for themselves.

Look, Father, at the young lady who is taking care of her man. Look deep inside her. Father can you see her pain as she struggles and doesn't know what to do.

Father, look at the mother or the father who has abandoned their kids. Father, do you see the impact that it has on this girl or boy? Do you see that they believe it is their fault?

Father, look at the divorced couple who now hate each other.

Father, look at the woman whose husband makes her feel inferior, not good enough.

Father, look at the boy or girl, lady or man, who was told that they were ignorant, dumb, and weren't going to be anything. Father, look at the hopelessness and the helplessness in them. Look at the ones who feel like they are failures. Do you see them?

Father, look at the depressed boy or girl who is so depressed that they have tried to take their lives.

Father, look at the husband who loves his wife and she doesn't love him anymore.

Now, father, look. Look at me, look at my heart, can you see my hurt, can you see my pain. Can you see the tears that have fallen from my eyes? Father, can you, can you hear what I am saying? Do you see what I am going through? Father, I tried my best, my very best, yet my best wasn't good enough. I depended on you and I trusted you, Lord Jesus. Yet, I feel as though I failed. It didn't end the way that I thought it would, I thought it would be a happy ending, but what is a happy ending? Am I fooled, am I being disillusioned? What, what, what was I thinking? Father, do you see?

Father, look at the families, look at the husbands, wives, sons and daughters, moms and dads. Look, Father, look. Look at the despair, the hopelessness, the hurt in their eyes, the loneliness that they feel. Look at them; they believe they have failed. Father, do you see?

Father, look at the mother and father who have lost their son or daughter; look at the child who has lost his mother, father, or brother, or sister. Look, at them, Lord. Do you see their pain, do you hear their cries, and do you see the emptiness and brokenness inside? Do you see, Father, do you see? Do you see their pain, Father, do you see?

Father, we need you, we need you like never before. The enemy is trying his best to get a stronghold on your sons and daughters. Father, we need you.

Father, your children, they are looking, they are searching, and they are being deceived along the way. What can I do; what can I say? Is there anything I can do or say that will make a difference?

I am crying for them, Lord Jesus, to come back home-- come back to where they belong. Come back!

Come, come, come back to Jesus, won't you? Father, do you see?

Ask the Lord Jesus to come into your heart and to forgive you of your sins. Salvation is a free gift; it is a free gift from God. Won't you try Jesus, the One who loves you just as you are?

That if you confess with your mouth the Lord Jesus and believe in your heart that God raised Him from the dead, you will be saved. For with the heart one believes unto righteousness and with the mouth confession is made unto salvation. For whoever believes on Him will not be put to shame (Romans 10:9-11).

Ask the Lord Jesus Christ to come into your heart, and to forgive you of your sins. Tell Him that you want to give your life over to Him; you want to experience His love for yourself.

Jesus is waiting. Won't you let Him heal you of your pain, your burdens, and your frustrations?

Broken- I Don't Think So!

All of you who are feeble kneed and feel faint stand up and rise!

Sheila was home alone doing her daily household chores. Her heart was burdened and heavy laden because of what she was going through. Sheila was going through a separation from her husband. All the pain felt like it was crushing her. She tried to be strong, she tried to pretend that all was well with her, but deep inside she was hurting and she was hurting bad. She would go to work and smile and say all the hellos to everyone, but all the time she was praying for strength for the day.

On her lunch break she would go out and walk. She would take this time to be alone with God. During this time she would cry out to the Lord, talk her problems out with the Lord, give her concerns and hurt to the Lord. She did this every day, for she knew where her strength came from. She would tell the Lord how unhappy she was, how she didn't want to go on, and that the pain was too much for her.

She loved her husband, but her husband, Reggie, was a selfish man, and only thought about himself. He put all of his needs before his wife, Sheila. It was all about him. He felt as if he was on top of the world. His business was doing well and he was making plenty of money. He felt as if he and his wife were going two separate ways, two separate paths, going in different directions. He no longer talked to her as he once did but now he talked at her. What a difference.

Sheila began to get tired of the situation and said, "I can't take it anymore, I tried in this marriage, and I gave it my all. Yet, that wasn't good enough. No matter what I did, Reggie still wanted a separation. Sheila was heartbroken, she cried, she felt helpless, hopeless, unattractive, and as if she wasn't good enough. She cried before the Lord and she stayed in His Word. She began to get busy in church. She attended Sunday service regularly and Bible study on Wednesday night. She said, "No matter what, I am going to serve the Lord. I choose to give this situation—this problem to the Lord. There's nothing I can do about it."

Sheila was a praying woman and she prayed not to become bitter or angry. She continued to stay in the Word. She decided to keep God first in her life; she knew He was faithful. The people at church knew something was going on in Sheila's life because she was now coming to church alone.

While Sheila continued to put God first, pursue Him, and seek Him, she began to get stronger; she felt better about herself and had more confidence. She didn't see Reggie very often, but Sheila was fine with that. She was doing more ministry than ever before. She felt joy and had joy in the midst of her circumstances.

Reggie stopped going to church. He thought he had it all together, everything was going his way. Even though he was separated, he now had a girlfriend. Oh, he thought this was the best thing that ever happened to him. He was the man, the big man on the block. He was making new friends and doing new things. He thought to himself, *I got it all together.*

Sheila began to think seriously about a divorce, she was feeling good about herself. One Sunday, a male church member approached her and wanted to talk to her. He introduced himself, and told her that his name was John. He also said, "I've been watching you and I noticed you come to church alone." He went on to say how he would like to take her out to lunch to get to know her.

Now Sheila was a good looking lady. She dressed nice, kept herself together; she had a beautiful personality, and was well liked. She really had herself together. More importantly, she was a woman of God. At the end of their conversation, John asked Sheila for her phone number. Sheila thought about her situation, where she was, and what she was becoming, and decided not to give John her number. Now, that didn't stop John. On Sundays he would make sure Sheila saw him, and he would still try to talk to her.

Meanwhile, Reggie couldn't help but to notice how Sheila was prospering. He knew God's hand was on his wife. You see, Reggie stopped going to church, he never put God first in his life, and his girlfriend did not attend church. Reggie knew he messed up and he messed up bad. His little happy world was not as happy any more. The grass wasn't as green as he thought it would be.

Sheila was in love with the Lord and it showed in and

through her life. As time went on, Reggie couldn't take it anymore. He broke things off with his girlfriend and even that was hard, because his girlfriend was not letting him go that easy. That became a battle. Reggie wanted to get back with Sheila and end the separation.

Sheila was not quite ready for that. She told Reggie, "Not now, I need more time. I am really happy with myself." She told Reggie, "You had broken me down, I felt crushed, I felt empty, and you left me feeling like nothing. Do you know what that feels like, to feel so empty? I worked hard in this marriage, and I gave you my all. I supported you in your business. When you were just starting off, I helped you with the books, I supported you, and I stood by you. You left me and you left me in a bad way, you left me for another woman, and now I am supposed to be glad or happy that you want this marriage to work. I don't think so! You hurt me and you hurt me bad. I had to pray and pray hard that bitterness or anger would not set in.

"When you left, after I was able to stop crying, stop questioning God, and finally stop the pity party, I said to myself, 'No more--never will a man be able to hurt me like you did. Never again. I will protect my heart, I will protect myself. I am not the same person that you left. I am all the stronger for it. I am better, I have my confidence back, and I am independent. I had to learn some things and give some things over to the Lord, and that's when I began to grow. That's when I let God minister to me. Over time, God picked me up and dusted me off. He gave me my joy back. He gave me a new love for myself. I love me, I love who I am."

I am somebody. Never think I will allow you to treat me

the way you did; those days are over with. I should have been stronger with you and demanded more from you. I learned that a man will only do what you allow him to do, and I allowed you to walk all over me. But not again, I don't think so!"

Sheila kept on, "Where is your little girlfriend? What happened, she got tired of you, and you thought you could waltz back into my world like nothing ever happened? I don't think so! What happened, she spent all your money, she wanted more from you, and you were not willing to give her more, or you wanted more from her, and she wasn't going for it? Oh, she found out how selfish you were, the real you came out, and I know the real her came out. You two deserve each other; you both are users. You left me, you left God, and your girlfriend became your god. Now you think I can just dismiss everything I've been through and run into your loving arms? I don't think so! Now your world is turned inside out; what does it feel like? Because you are in trouble with your business and have no money, you come to me. I don't think so!

"Look at you, look where you are. You don't have a clue. I was the best thing that ever happened to you and you got trapped in the arms of another woman who pretended to be what you thought you wanted. I am not mad or angry; I had to give all that to the Lord for my sake. Yes, I had hard times, it was rough. But I made it! I realized that I made it because of Jesus, not in my own strength, but in the power of the Lord. I made it!"

"I am a different person, I love me, I love what God has made me to become. I am going to tell you what you need to do; first off, you haven't truly repented. You just said you wanted me to come back to you. I am not that gullible any-more; I am not that woman anymore. You need to repent to God and ask Him to forgive you and try to find Jesus for your-self, because I can't help you; that's something you have to do on your own and for yourself.

"The time is not right for us to get back together. You know, Reggie, I loved you, I respected you, but you were not man enough to come and talk to me and tell me you wanted out. Not until you had made all your plans with your little girlfriend. You got caught up in the thrill, in the sneaking around, and thinking you were invincible.

But it's time for me to just do me; I don't want to go back to the way things were. I love me, where I am in life, and the relationship that I have with the Lord. Since our separation, He has blessed me in ways that you can't understand. When my heart was broken He was close to me. He is the one that has kept me through it all. Oh no, I can't go backwards, I must continue to move forward. I've learned to put the Lord first, do ministry, keep myself busy, and I am blessed for it.

You want me to get back with you? Oh no, I don't think so!

Ask for His Help (Salvation)

Ask the Lord Jesus to come into your heart and to forgive you of your sins. Salvation is a free gift; it is a free gift from God. Won't you try Jesus, the One who loves you just as you are?

"That if you confess with your mouth the Lord Jesus and believe in your heart that God raised Him from the dead, you will be saved. For with the heart one believes unto righteousness and with the mouth confession is made unto salvation. For whoever believes on Him will not be put to shame" (Romans 10:9-11).

Ask the Lord Jesus Christ to come into your heart, and to forgive you of your sins. Tell Him that you want to give your life over to Him; you want to experience His love for yourself.

Jesus is waiting, won't you let Him heal you of your pain, your burdens, and your frustrations.

No matter what you have been through, or if you think you are not good enough, or you keep telling yourself you have to clean yourself up before you come to the Lord. That's not true,

Jesus wants you to come to Him just as you are. Won't you try Him and let Him love on you.

Always remember Jesus loves you. There isn't anything you can do to keep him from loving you. Come to Him just as you are.

Jesus loves you! Yes, you.

CPSIA information can be obtained at www.ICGtesting.com
Printed in the USA
LVOW101018060712

289008LV00001B/4/P